Exploring American History 2

Reading, Vocabulary, and Test-taking Skills

Phil LeFaivre

Flo Decker

McGraw-Hill
ESL/ELT

Exploring American History 2: Reading, Vocabulary, and Test-taking Skills

Published by McGraw-Hill ESL/ELT, a business unit of the McGraw-Hill Companies, Inc., 1221 Avenue of the Americas, New York, NY 10020.

ISBN: 0-07-285464-2

Editorial director: Tina Carver

Executive editor: Erik Gundersen

Developmental editor: Stephen Handorf

Editorial assistant: David Averbach

Production manager: Juanita Thompson

Photo researcher: Tobi Zausner

Cover design: Four Lakes Colorgraphics Inc.

Interior design: Acento Visual

Art: Wilkinson Studios

Maps: Mapping Specialists

Photo credits: Page 1 © Hulton Archive; Page 3 © Kim Kullish/CORBIS Saba; Page 7 © NASM; Page 15 © Bettman/CORBIS; Page 16 © Bettman/CORBIS; Page 17 © Richard Berenholtz/CORBIS; Page 21 © Bettman/CORBIS; Page 22 © CORBIS; Page 29 © Hulton Archive; Page 30 © Bettman/CORBIS; Page 35 © Dorothea Lange/The Oakland Museum of California; Page 36 © Dorothea Lange/The Oakland Museum of California; Page 37 © Dorothea Lange/The Oakland Museum of California; Page 43 © Bettman/CORBIS; Page 44 © Hulton Archive; Page 45 © Associated Press/US Postal Service; Page 49 © Bettman/CORBIS; Page 51 © Michael T. Sedam/CORBIS; Page 57 © Bettman/CORBIS; Page 58 © James L. Amos/CORBIS; Page 63 © CORBIS; Page 65 © Instructional Resources Corporation; Page 71 © Hulton Archive/Getty Images; Page 72 © Robert W. Kelley/Time Life Pictures/Getty Images; Page 77 © NASA; Page 79 © NASA; Page 85 © Owen Franken/CORBIS; Page 86 © Instructional Resources Corporation; Page 91 © Phillip James Corwin/CORBIS; Page 93 © Bettman/CORBIS; Page 99 © Getty Images; Page 101 © Bettman/CORBIS; Page 105 © N.Y. Newswire/Sands/CORBIS Sygma; Page 106 © AP/Wide World Photos.

Acknowledgements

The publisher and authors would like to thank the following educational professionals whose comments, reviews, and assistance were instrumental in the development of *Exploring American History:*

Debbie Barshay, *Bridgewater State University* (Bridgewater, MA)

Claire Bonskowski, *Fairfax County Public Schools* (Fairfax, VA)

Greg Keech, *City College of San Francisco, Downtown Campus* (San Francisco, CA)

Maryann Lyons, *Francisco Middle School* (San Francisco, CA)

Sue Nordberg, *Old Orchard Junior High School, School District 68* (Skokie, IL)

Meredith Pike-Baky, *Education Task Force* (Marin County, CA)

Stephen Sloan, *James Monroe High School* (North Hills, CA)

Leslie Eloise Somers, *Miami-Dade County Public Schools* (Miami, FL)

Phil LeFaivre would also like to thank Laurel Mays Ostermeier, *Parkway School District* (St. Louis, MO), for research assistance.

Scope and Sequence

Chapter & Title	Topic	Reading Skill	Academic Vocabulary
1 **Ellis Island: A Door to Opportunity** *Page 1*	European immigrants arrive at Ellis Island to begin building new lives in America. *1892 – 1924*	Previewing	**Communities** resident rural suburban urban
2 **The Wright Brothers and the Birth of Flight** *Page 7*	Two brothers from Ohio build and fly the first engine-powered airplane. *1900 – 1903*	Asking Yourself Questions	**Geometry** angle horizontal parallel vertical
Workshop I: Word Power **Number Prefixes** • Guessing word meanings based on number prefixes *Page 13*			
3 **The San Francisco Earthquake** *Page 15*	San Francisco, California, is nearly destroyed by the worst natural disaster in American history. *1906*	Visualizing	**Earthquakes** fault geology magnitude Richter Scale
4 **Women Win the Right to Vote** *Page 21*	American women fight for 70 years to be allowed to vote in the United States. *1848 – 1918*	Using Context Clues	**The Right to Vote** campaign candidate majority primary election
Workshop II: Test-Taking Strategies **Reading Comprehension Tests** • Making inferences • *Practice Test* *Page 27*			

<table>
<tr><th>Chapter & Title</th><th>Topic</th><th>Reading Skill</th><th>Academic Vocabulary</th></tr>
<tr><td>5
The Jazz Age

Page 29</td><td>African Americans invent a new kind of music, and the whole country goes wild.

1920 – 1929</td><td>Noticing Cause and Effect</td><td>Music
harmony
rhythm
solo
trio</td></tr>
<tr><td>6
Dorothea Lange: Photographer of the Great Depression

Page 35</td><td>The United States goes through the worst economic period in its history, and Dorothea Lange records it in pictures.

1929 – 1936</td><td>Separating Facts from Opinions</td><td>Money and Banking
deposit
inflation
interest
withdraw</td></tr>
<tr><td colspan="4">Workshop III: Word Power
Suffixes
• Making new words
• Recognizing parts of speech
Page 41</td></tr>
<tr><td>7
Jesse Owens: The Fastest Man

Page 43</td><td>Jesse Owens, an amazing African-American athlete, shows the world that Adolph Hitler is wrong.

1936</td><td>Noticing the Sequence of Events</td><td>World War II
fascism
genocide
ghetto
stereotype</td></tr>
<tr><td>8
Pearl Harbor, December 7, 1941

Page 49</td><td>The United States is attacked without warning and starts fighting in World War II.

1941</td><td>Noticing Details</td><td>Diplomacy
ally
ambassador
liberate
neutral</td></tr>
<tr><td colspan="4">Workshop IV: Test-Taking Strategies
Vocabulary Tests
• Choosing the best word to complete a sentence
• Practice Test
Page 55</td></tr>
</table>

Chapter & Title	Topic	Reading Skill	Academic Vocabulary
9 **Cesar Chavez and the United Farm Workers** *Page 57*	Cesar Chavez, a Mexican-American farm worker, fights grape growers to improve working conditions for all farm workers. *1962 – 1975*	Finding Main Ideas and Supporting Details	**Business and Labor** activist capitalism fringe benefit seniority
10 **The Cuban Missile Crisis** *Page 63*	The Soviet Union puts missiles in Cuba, and the world comes close to nuclear war. *1962*	Noticing the Sequence of Events	**War and Peace** alliance blockade diplomacy superpower
Workshop V: Word Power **Word Parts and Meanings** • Recognizing common roots and word parts • Guessing word meanings *Page 69*			
11 **Martin Luther King, Jr.'s Dream** *Page 71*	Martin Luther King, Jr., an African-American minister from Alabama, leads the fight to protect the rights of Americans of all races. *1954 – 1963*	Making Inferences	**The Civil Rights Movement** integrate Jim Crow segregation sit-in
12 **The Race to the Moon** *Page 77*	The United States races against the Soviet Union to be the first to send a man to the moon. *1961 – 1969*	Noticing Cause and Effect	**Space Travel** lunar navigate orbit satellite
Workshop VI: Test-Taking Strategies **Reading Tests** • Noticing key words like *best, same, opposite, not,* and *most* • *Practice Test* *Page 83*			

Chapter & Title	Topic	Reading Skill	Academic Vocabulary
13 **Watergate** *Page 85*	President Richard Nixon is caught lying to the country and decides to resign. *1972 – 1974*	Separating Facts from Opinions	**The U.S. Constitution** impeach repeal term veto
14 **Remembering the Vietnam War** *Page 91*	The United States builds a memorial to honor soldiers killed in Vietnam and help the country heal. *1973 – 1982*	Summarizing	**Military Abbreviations** AWOL GI MIA POW
Workshop VII: Word Power **Idioms** • Guessing the meaning of common idioms from context *Page 97*			
15 **The End of the Cold War** *Page 99*	The Berlin Wall comes down and ends the Cold War between the United States and the Soviet Union. *1961 – 1989*	Summarizing	**The Free Enterprise System** corporation credit dividend revenue
16 **The Attack on the World Trade Center** *Page 105*	Terrorists attack the United States and change the way Americans think about the world. *2001 – 2003*	Making Inferences	**Terrorism and International Conflicts** coalition evacuate hijack sanctions
Workshop VIII: Test-Taking Strategies **Vocabulary Tests** • Choosing one word to complete two sentences • *Practice Test* *Page 111*			

Introduction

Exploring American History is a two-book series, that develops students' reading, vocabulary-building, and test-taking skills around compelling topics in U.S. history. In school settings, English-language learners are expected to learn mainstream content in the English language as they are acquiring knowledge of the language itself. *Exploring American History* has been developed to assist learners in this overwhelming task by using controlled vocabulary and grammatical structures and providing extensive language support. Engaging historical topics have been selected to give students a general overview of American history. The readings are written in a comprehensible narrative format and supported by artwork that enables students to visualize specific artifacts, geographical locations, events, and modern-day connections. As students are introduced to historical concepts, they are taught vocabulary, reading comprehension skills and strategies, and test-taking skills. The books thus serve as an on-ramp to the academic language skills needed in an American classroom.

Components

The complete *Exploring American History* program includes the following components:

- Student Book 1 (prehistory – 1865), high beginning
- Student Book 2 (1892 – present), low intermediate
- Teacher's Manuals 1 and 2 featuring:
    - Chapter quizzes
    - Answer keys to exercises and quizzes
- Audiocassette/CD 1 and 2 with recordings of all reading passages

Each Student Book contains 16 six-page chapters designed to help students improve their reading comprehension and vocabulary-building skills. The readings in each chapter are 400–440 words long. In addition, there are eight two-page Workshops that help students increase their word power and improve their test-taking skills. The two-page Workshops appear after each even-numbered chapter. At the end of each book are a full glossary and pronunciation key for target vocabulary, a skills index, and answers to practice tests. Each book also includes on the inside back cover a full-color historical map of the United States showing all places mentioned in the text.

Guide to Exploring American History

Chapter Opening Art
Photos and art reproductions introduce students visually to the topic of the reading.

Get Ready to Read
1. Topics for small group discussions enable students to interact with classmates as they activate their background knowledge.
2. Students make a prediction about information they will find in the reading.

Audiocassette/CD Icon
Recordings of each reading selection assist students with an aural/oral learning style preference.

Key Vocabulary Items
Six words in each reading are highlighted with bold-faced type. Students study these in the *Build Your Vocabulary* activity.

Map Icon
This icon in the margin indicates that a place name in the reading appears on the U.S. map on the inside back cover of the book.

Artwork
Maps, photos, and illustrations provide visual aids. These graphics facilitate reading comprehension.

Numbered Lines
Every fifth line is numbered for easy reference.

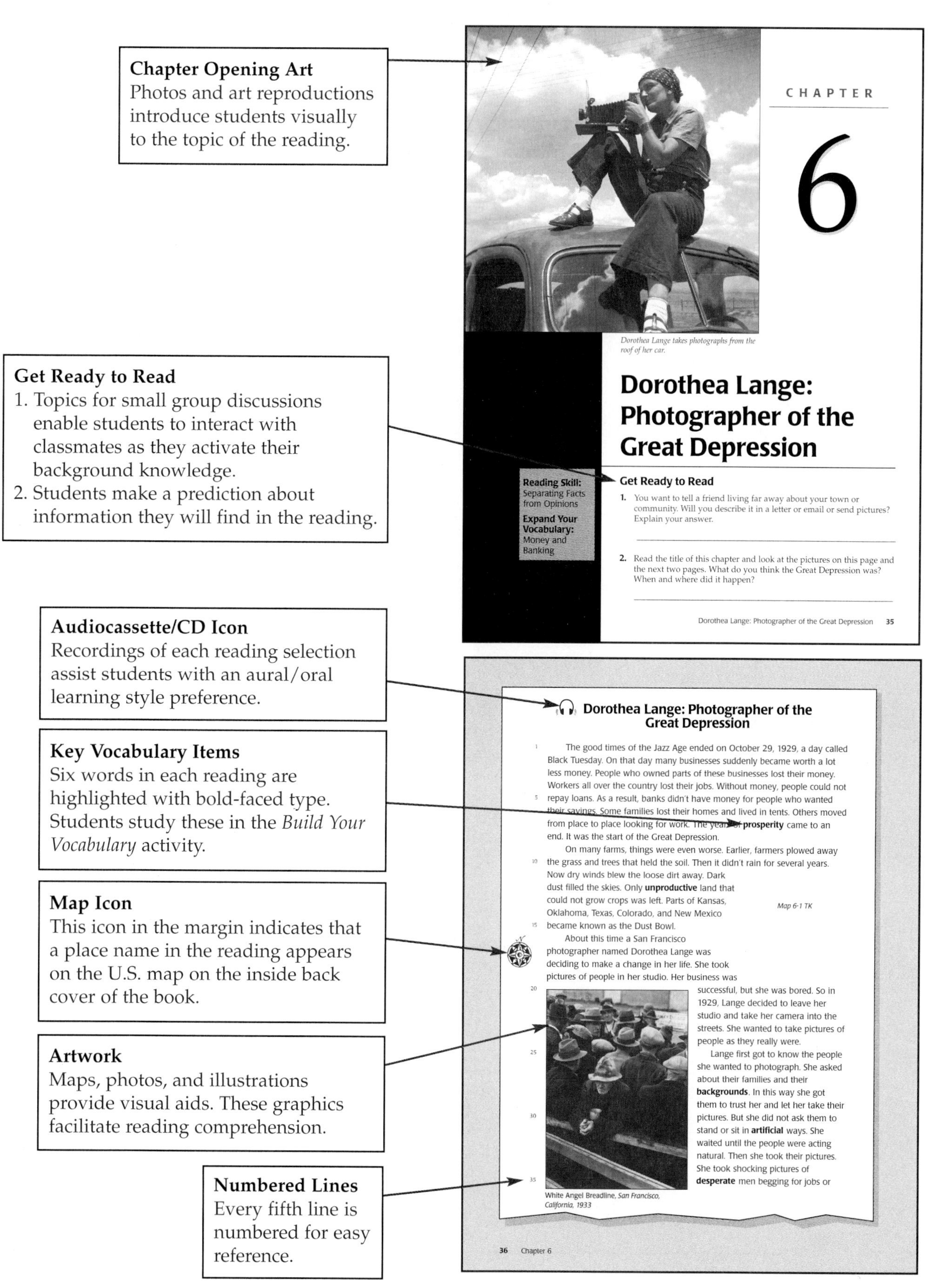

CHAPTER

6

Dorothea Lange takes photographs from the roof of her car.

Dorothea Lange: Photographer of the Great Depression

Reading Skill: Separating Facts from Opinions

Expand Your Vocabulary: Money and Banking

Get Ready to Read

1. You want to tell a friend living far away about your town or community. Will you describe it in a letter or email or send pictures? Explain your answer.

2. Read the title of this chapter and look at the pictures on this page and the next two pages. What do you think the Great Depression was? When and where did it happen?

Dorothea Lange: Photographer of the Great Depression 35

Dorothea Lange: Photographer of the Great Depression

The good times of the Jazz Age ended on October 29, 1929, a day called Black Tuesday. On that day many businesses suddenly became worth a lot less money. People who owned parts of these businesses lost their money. Workers all over the country lost their jobs. Without money, people could not repay loans. As a result, banks didn't have money for people who wanted their savings. Some families lost their homes and lived in tents. Others moved from place to place looking for work. The years of **prosperity** came to an end. It was the start of the Great Depression.

On many farms, things were even worse. Earlier, farmers plowed away the grass and trees that held the soil. Then it didn't rain for several years. Now dry winds blew the loose dirt away. Dark dust filled the skies. Only **unproductive** land that could not grow crops was left. Parts of Kansas, Oklahoma, Texas, Colorado, and New Mexico became known as the Dust Bowl.

Map 6-1 TK

About this time a San Francisco photographer named Dorothea Lange was deciding to make a change in her life. She took pictures of people in her studio. Her business was successful, but she was bored. So in 1929, Lange decided to leave her studio and take her camera into the streets. She wanted to take pictures of people as they really were.

Lange first got to know the people she wanted to photograph. She asked about their families and their **backgrounds**. In this way she got them to trust her and let her take their pictures. But she did not ask them to stand or sit in **artificial** ways. She waited until the people were acting natural. Then she took their pictures. She took shocking pictures of **desperate** men begging for jobs or

White Angel Breadline, *San Francisco, California, 1933*

36 Chapter 6

standing in long lines to get a cup of soup. Her photographs told the story of the Great Depression better than words could.

The government hired Lange to report on the living conditions of families from the Dust Bowl. During this time she took her most famous photograph, *Migrant Mother*. It is a picture of a tired mother and her starving children on a farm. The mother's face shows a mixture of worry and **determination**, the strength to go on. This picture appeared in many newspapers and caused the government to send 20,000 pounds of food to her farm.

Lange did not think of herself as an artist. Even so, three months after her death in 1965, her photographs were shown at the Museum of Modern Art in New York. Today her photographs are in the Oakland Museum of California.

Migrant Mother, *Nipomo, California, 1936*

Check Your Understanding

1. Why did farmlands turn to dust and blow away in 1929?

2. Why did Dorothea Lange get to know the people before she photographed them?

The reading selection says that Lange's photographs tell a story. What story does the photograph called *White Angel Breadline* tell?

Check Your Understanding
These questions provide students with an opportunity to assess their own understanding of the reading.

Light Bulb Icon
This icon indicates that the question requires a higher degree of critical thinking, inference, or analysis.

Build Your Vocabulary

What is the meaning of each word in red? Fill in the correct bubble.

1. Some families lost their homes and lived in tents. Others moved from place to place looking for work. The years of **prosperity** came to an end.
   - (A) anger and hate
   - (B) poverty and hunger
   - (C) success and money
   - (D) crime

2. Now dry winds blew the loose dirt away. Dark dust filled the skies. Only **unproductive** land that could not grow crops was left.
   - (A) beautiful
   - (B) easy to sell
   - (C) dangerous
   - (D) unable to bring good results

3. Lange first got to know the people she wanted to photograph. She asked about their families and their **backgrounds**. In this way she got them to trust her and let her take their pictures.
   - (A) past and present life
   - (B) amount of money in banks
   - (C) favorite foods
   - (D) knowledge of photography

4. But she did not ask them to stand or sit in some **artificial** way. She waited until the people were acting natural.
   - (A) unnatural
   - (B) exciting
   - (C) stupid
   - (D) loud

5. She took shocking pictures of **desperate** men begging for jobs or standing in long lines to get a cup of soup.
   - (A) strong and active
   - (B) needing something badly
   - (C) strange or unusual
   - (D)

6. The mother's face shows a mixture of worry and **determination**, the strength to go on.
   - (A) hopelessness about the future
   - (B) hunger
   - (C) happiness
   - (D) strong desire to continue trying

Build Your Vocabulary
Each of the six bold-faced words from the reading are included in this activity.

Excerpts from the Reading
Relevant parts of the reading are reprinted here to provide context clues.

Multiple Choice Responses
This activity models a standardized-test format to familiarize students with the concept of "bubbling in" their test answers.

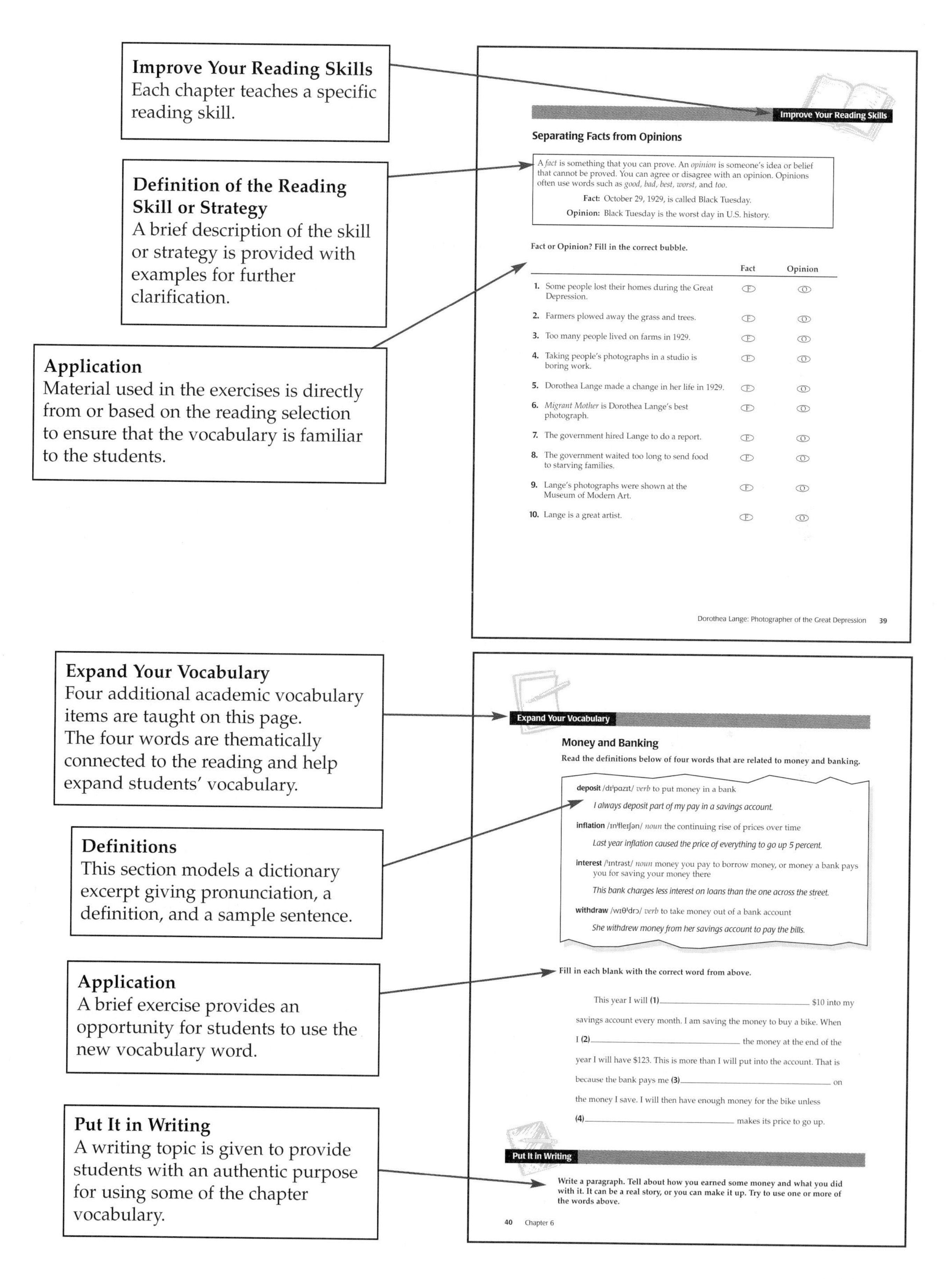

Improve Your Reading Skills
Each chapter teaches a specific reading skill.

Definition of the Reading Skill or Strategy
A brief description of the skill or strategy is provided with examples for further clarification.

Application
Material used in the exercises is directly from or based on the reading selection to ensure that the vocabulary is familiar to the students.

Improve Your Reading Skills

Separating Facts from Opinions

A *fact* is something that you can prove. An *opinion* is someone's idea or belief that cannot be proved. You can agree or disagree with an opinion. Opinions often use words such as *good, bad, best, worst,* and *too.*

Fact: October 29, 1929, is called Black Tuesday.

Opinion: Black Tuesday is the worst day in U.S. history.

Fact or Opinion? Fill in the correct bubble.

	Fact	Opinion
1. Some people lost their homes during the Great Depression.	Ⓕ	Ⓞ
2. Farmers plowed away the grass and trees.	Ⓕ	Ⓞ
3. Too many people lived on farms in 1929.	Ⓕ	Ⓞ
4. Taking people's photographs in a studio is boring work.	Ⓕ	Ⓞ
5. Dorothea Lange made a change in her life in 1929.	Ⓕ	Ⓞ
6. *Migrant Mother* is Dorothea Lange's best photograph.	Ⓕ	Ⓞ
7. The government hired Lange to do a report.	Ⓕ	Ⓞ
8. The government waited too long to send food to starving families.	Ⓕ	Ⓞ
9. Lange's photographs were shown at the Museum of Modern Art.	Ⓕ	Ⓞ
10. Lange is a great artist.	Ⓕ	Ⓞ

Dorothea Lange: Photographer of the Great Depression 39

Expand Your Vocabulary
Four additional academic vocabulary items are taught on this page. The four words are thematically connected to the reading and help expand students' vocabulary.

Definitions
This section models a dictionary excerpt giving pronunciation, a definition, and a sample sentence.

Application
A brief exercise provides an opportunity for students to use the new vocabulary word.

Put It in Writing
A writing topic is given to provide students with an authentic purpose for using some of the chapter vocabulary.

Expand Your Vocabulary

Money and Banking

Read the definitions below of four words that are related to money and banking.

deposit /dɪˈpɑzɪt/ *verb* to put money in a bank
I always deposit part of my pay in a savings account.

inflation /ɪnˈfleɪʃən/ *noun* the continuing rise of prices over time
Last year inflation caused the price of everything to go up 5 percent.

interest /ˈɪntrəst/ *noun* money you pay to borrow money, or money a bank pays you for saving your money there
This bank charges less interest on loans than the one across the street.

withdraw /wɪθˈdrɔ/ *verb* to take money out of a bank account
She withdrew money from her savings account to pay the bills.

Fill in each blank with the correct word from above.

This year I will **(1)**__________ $10 into my savings account every month. I am saving the money to buy a bike. When I **(2)**__________ the money at the end of the year I will have $123. This is more than I will put into the account. That is because the bank pays me **(3)**__________ on the money I save. I will then have enough money for the bike unless **(4)**__________ makes its price to go up.

Put It in Writing

Write a paragraph. Tell about how you earned some money and what you did with it. It can be a real story, or you can make it up. Try to use one or more of the words above.

40 Chapter 6

Tips for the Teacher

Get Ready to Read

The first question in each *Get Ready to Read* activity activates students' background knowledge—a critical factor in developing their ability to comprehend a reading passage. Whenever possible, have students discuss their answers in small groups. This gives students an authentic purpose for listening and speaking, while helping them extend their ideas in an environment that is less threatening than a class-wide discussion. The second question asks students to make predictions about what they will be reading. Be careful not to stress the accuracy of the prediction—the purpose is to give students a focus as they read.

The first chapter of each book includes a previewing activity, which allows students to discover the organizational pattern of the chapter. Repeat this activity at the beginning of subsequent chapters until students have internalized the chapter components. This will help them feel more confident as they proceed through the book.

You might also like to have students practice skimming and scanning skills before reading. To practice *scanning*, give students one minute to look through the reading and circle all the dates or proper nouns. To practice *skimming*, allow students to read the *Check Your Understanding* questions at the end of the reading. Then give them five minutes to quickly skim through the reading to look for the answers. Follow this with a more careful reading.

Reading

Play the audiocassette or CD as the students read the words silently in their Student Books. This will enable them to hear how the words are pronounced and grouped by a native English speaker. In addition, this will force the students to progress through the entire passage without worrying about the meaning of individual words. If possible, do not stop the cassette or CD to answer questions because it will interrupt the flow of the passage. After the students have heard the entire passage, the audio can be used in smaller segments as needed. Students can then discuss each section within a small group before proceeding to the next segment.

Check Your Understanding

These questions should not be treated as a test but as a self-assessment tool or an invitation to students to explore the reading more thoroughly. Have students work alone or with a partner as they revisit the reading to locate the answers.

Build Your Vocabulary

Students may work in pairs or small groups to discuss the information as they choose the correct meaning for each word. This activity should not be treated as a vocabulary test since students need time to learn the vocabulary before being tested. The use of context clues is explicitly taught and practiced in Chapter 4. However, it is recommended that you encourage students to use these techniques in each chapter.

Improve Your Reading Skills

Language learners' tendency to read word by word complicates their ability to comprehend a reading. To help students break this habit and become more effective readers, *Exploring American History* teaches them to interact with each passage by visualizing the passage in their minds, questioning it as they read, and making personal connections to it. These specific strategies are each presented only once in each of the Student Books. However, it is suggested you model these strategies with each reading passage until you feel confident that your students demonstrate the ability to proceed independently.

Expand Your Vocabulary

Students should read the dictionary entries first. You can model pronunciations. Then have students work with a partner or in small groups to discuss their choices in the application exercises.

Put It in Writing

This activity is designed to give students production practice and tie together what they have learned. When reading the first drafts of students' paragraphs, focus on the content of their paragraph and the use of vocabulary, not on the grammatical form.

Workshops

Word Power Workshops give students a chance to explore aspects of the English language that are not dealt with in the readings. These activities can be done alone, in pairs, in small groups, or as homework, according to what you feel is most appropriate. *Test-Taking Strategies Workshops* introduce students to a variety of standardized test types that they are likely to encounter. Have students complete the sample questions and discuss the answers as a class before completing the practice tests on their own. Answers to these tests can be found on page 122.

To the Student

Welcome to *Exploring American History.* Before you begin to use this book, it's a good idea to get to know what is in it. Do the following activity to learn about the different parts of your book.

1. Open to the first page of this book. This is the title page. What information can you find on this page? Put a check (✔) next to each thing that you find there:

_____ The title of the book

_____ The names of the authors

_____ The name of the publishing company

_____ The date the book was published

2. Turn to the Scope and Sequence on pages iv–vii.

a. How many chapters are in this book? _____

b. How many pages are in Chapter 8? _____

c. What page does Chapter 10 begin on? _____

3. The first page of each chapter begins with a large picture. Look at all 16 of them. Choose your favorite. Form groups of two or three and share your ideas.

4. The Glossary begins on page 113. What information is in the Glossary?

____

____

5. Find the word *boycott* in the Glossary.

a. What chapter is it used in? _____

b. What other information about *boycott* did you find?

____

6. Look at the list of states, abbreviations, and capitals on pages 117 and 118.

a. What is the abbreviation of Idaho? _____

b. What is the capital of Vermont? ________________________________

7. What do you find on the inside back cover? ____________________________

We hope you will enjoy using this book and learning about the history of the United States.

New immigrants on a ship to Ellis Island in New York Harbor around 1900

CHAPTER

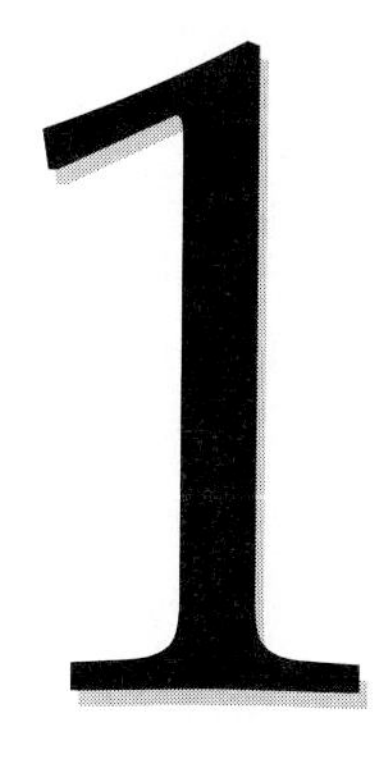

Ellis Island: A Door to Opportunity

Reading Skill: Previewing

Expand Your Vocabulary: Communities

Get Ready to Read

1. You decide to move to a new country, and you can take only one suitcase. What will you pack? Why?

Items I will pack	Reason for packing them
photo album	I want to have pictures of my family and friends.

2. What are immigrants? Look at the picture above and read the title of this chapter. Where do you think these immigrants came from? What kinds of opportunities do you think they wanted? Do you think they found them?

____

____

Ellis Island: A Door to Opportunity

The United States is a nation of immigrants. These immigrants come to the United States from every part of the world. Many of them bring only what they can carry in a box or suitcase. They give up everything else for the chance to make better lives for themselves in America.

From 1892 to 1924 the first thing most European immigrants saw was a small island in New York Harbor called Ellis Island.* More than 20 million people got off crowded ships there, and many began the long, often difficult job of becoming Americans. Each of these **newcomers** was asked to give his or her name. An official then said the name and copied it on an **application** for entry into the United States. Sometimes the official had trouble saying or spelling people's names. But the newcomers usually said nothing. As a result, some family names and their spellings were changed forever. For example, the German name *Mueller* sometimes became *Miller.*

Next, a doctor examined each person. An illness or physical problem could **disqualify** someone from entering the country. So people tried to hide unhealthy legs under long coats and dresses. Some people were told to cough into a handkerchief. Doctors checked it for blood. Blood was a sign of a serious illness that could keep someone out of the country. Often the newcomers failed the test. One in five people was kept and asked more questions or sent back home.

Even after the immigrants were allowed into the United States, life was difficult. Most of them spoke little or no English. Few of them had money. Some Americans didn't like these new immigrants and **refused** to give them jobs. So they had to help each other. Italian, Irish, and Jewish immigrants joined together to form **communities**. They opened stores, published newspapers, and cared for one another. They wanted to make a better life for themselves in this land of opportunity. As time passed, many immigrants **migrated** west to work on farms and in factories, start new businesses, and become skilled workers.

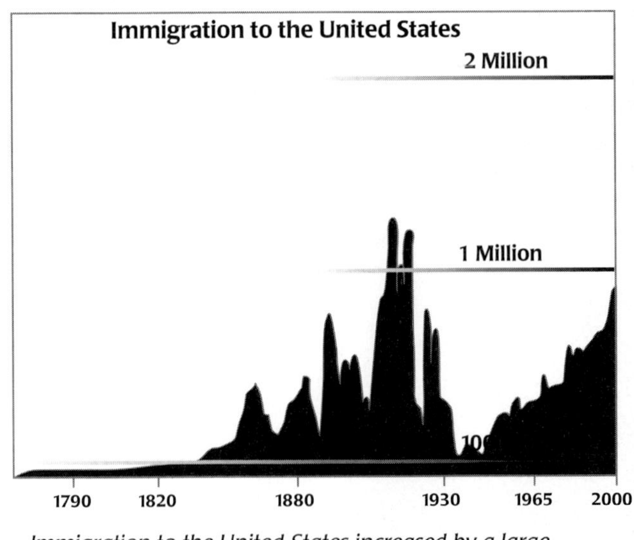

Immigration to the United States increased by a large amount between 1880 and 1930. Many of the immigrants came through Ellis Island.

* See the map on the inside back cover for the location of Ellis Island in the United States.

Ellis Island closed in 1954, but the United States still welcomes many new immigrants every year. Thousands of people from Mexico and Central America have moved to the southwestern part of the United States. Vietnamese, Korean, Filipino, and Chinese immigrants arrive daily on the West Coast. Many Cubans have entered Florida to escape problems in their homeland. All of these newcomers have one thing in common: they are looking for a better life. As they build their new lives, they make America a better nation.

Immigrants from around the world become U.S. citizens.

Check Your Understanding

1. When officials wrote immigrants' names incorrectly, why didn't the immigrants correct them?

They wanted to enter the United States, and they didn't want to cause problems.

2. Why did doctors examine the immigrants?

____

____

3. Why did immigrants from different countries join together to form their own separate groups in the United States?

____

____

Build Your Vocabulary

What is the meaning of each word in red? Fill in the correct bubble. The first one has been done for you.

1. More than 20 million people got off crowded ships there, and many began the long, often difficult job of becoming Americans. Each of these **newcomers** was asked to give his or her name.

   - (●) people who have just arrived
   - (B) doctors
   - (C) government officials
   - (D) people who live in New York

2. An official then said the name and copied it on an **application** for entry into the United States.

   - (A) ticket to ride a train
   - (B) form that you write on to ask for something
   - (C) newspaper
   - (D) list of someone's things

3. An illness or physical problem could **disqualify** someone from entering the country.

   - (A) ask someone to do something
   - (B) hurt someone very badly
   - (C) make someone move quickly
   - (D) prevent someone from doing something because of a rule

4. Italian, Irish, and Jewish immigrants joined together to form **communities**. They opened stores, published newspapers, and cared for one another.

   - (A) groups of people who live together
   - (B) businesses
   - (C) newspapers
   - (D) Italian, Irish, and Jewish people

5. Some Americans didn't like these new immigrants and **refused** to give them jobs.

   - (A) explained the reasons for doing something
   - (B) offered money
   - (C) agreed to do something
   - (D) said that they were not going to do something

6. As time passed, many immigrants **migrated** west to work on farms and in factories, start new businesses, and become skilled workers.

   - (A) joined
   - (B) moved
   - (C) looked
   - (D) read about

Previewing

It's a good idea to *preview* material you are planning to read. To preview, "skim" the new reading selection or chapter. In other words, look through it but don't read every word. Instead, look for things that quickly give you ideas about what the reading or chapter will be about.

"Preview" this chapter and answer the questions below.

1. Look at the chapter title and the pictures on pages 1–3. What do they tell you about the reading selection?

People come to the United States for opportunity...

____

2. How many pages are in this chapter? __________

3. What is the name of the activity before the reading selection on page 1? Why is this activity important?

____

4. How many words appear in **red** in the reading selection on pages 2–3?

____

5. What is the name of the activity just after the reading selection on page 3? Why is this activity important?

____

____

6. Where do the words in the ***Build Your Vocabulary*** activity on page 4 come from?

____

7. How many words are in the ***Expand Your Vocabulary*** activity on page 6? Do you think that these are easy or difficult words? __________

8. What are you asked to do in the final activity of the chapter?

____

Remember to preview each chapter in this book *before* you read it. Previewing will help you know what to expect when you read.

Expand Your Vocabulary

Communities

Read the definitions below of four words that are related to places to live and work.

resident /ˈrɛzɪdənt/ *noun* a person who lives in a particular place

She has been a resident of this town for several years.

rural /ˈrurəl/ *adjective* relating to the countryside

Neighbors in rural areas sometimes live far apart.

suburban /səˈbɜrbən/ *adjective* relating to towns near a large city

The workers drive into the city from many suburban towns.

urban /ˈɜrbən/ *adjective* relating to a city

Sidewalks in urban areas are often crowded with people.

Fill in each blank with the correct word from above.

1. Subways carry people from jobs in the city to the ____________________ areas where they live.

2. Driving can be very slow on crowded ____________________ streets.

3. My uncle is a(n) ____________________ of Austin, Texas.

4. The ____________________ road ran between miles of corn and wheat fields.

Put It in Writing

Write a paragraph about the community in which you live. Tell about the people, the homes or apartments, and any shops. Try to use one or more of the words above.

CHAPTER

Wilbur and Orville Wright's plane lifts from a wooden rail and flies for the first time on December 17, 1903.

The Wright Brothers and the Birth of Flight

Reading Skill:
Asking Yourself Questions

Expand Your Vocabulary:
Geometry

Get Ready to Read

1. Why do you think people in 1900 wanted to build a machine to fly in?

____

____

2. What problems do you think the builders of the first airplane had? How do you think they solved them?

____

____

The Wright Brothers and the Birth of Flight

1 A letter with a strange **request** arrived at the U.S. Weather Bureau in 1900. A bicycle maker in Dayton, Ohio, was asking for a list of windy places. He also wanted the places to have lots of water or sand. The letter was signed by Wilbur Wright. There was a reason that he wanted this unusual list. 5 Wilbur and his brother, Orville, had a machine they thought could fly.* It needed a strong wind to help it get off the ground. But they also wanted water or soft sand in case it crashed. The Weather Bureau gave them a list. The brothers chose Kitty Hawk, North Carolina. It was an **isolated** area far from large towns. There 10 were few trees there, and there was plenty of sand.

The Wright Brothers were not the first people to try to fly. Several 15 inventors flew gliders without engines before, but they were never able to control the flight. The wind blew the gliders in 20 all directions. The pilots were helpless. Injuries and even **fatalities** were common.

The Wright Brothers 25 thought they had a **solution** to the problem. By moving the wings and the tail, a pilot could control the plane. The Wrights tried out more than 200 wings and tails on 30 gliders until they found a **combination** that worked. Then they built an engine and **experimented** with propellers.

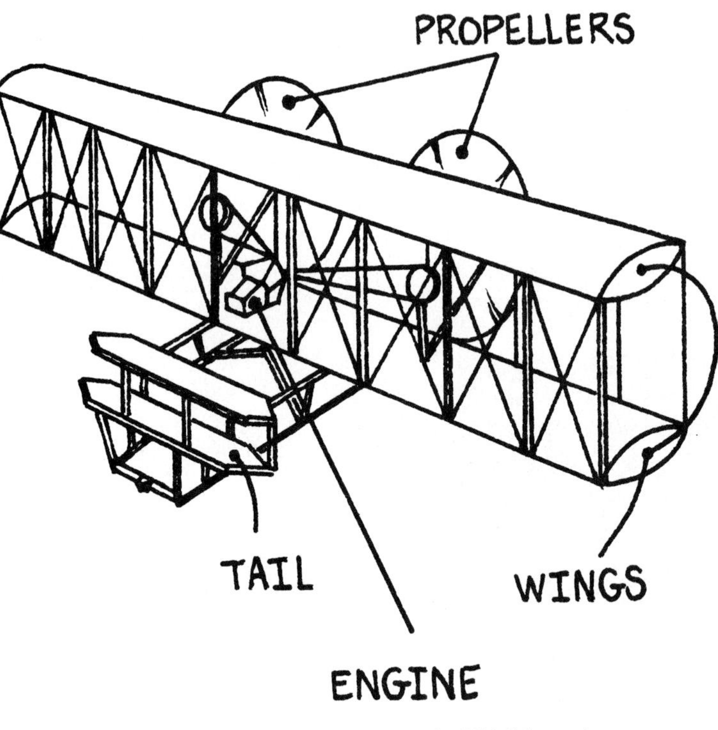

An airplane like the one the Wrights used

In the autumn of 1903, the Wright Brothers took their airplane in pieces to Kitty Hawk. They put it together there and tested the engine. The plane was supposed to roll down a 60-foot wooden rail into the wind. Then if they 35 were lucky the airplane was going to fly into the sky.

* See the map on the inside back cover for the location of Dayton, Ohio, and Kitty Hawk, North Carolina, in the United States.

Their first try on December 14 failed. The engine stopped working and the plane was damaged. It took three days to repair the plane. Then the weather became cold and very windy. But they could not wait any longer. On December 17, five men moved the 600-pound (272-kilogram) plane over
40 frozen sand to the wooden rail. The engine started. The propellers began to turn, and the strange machine moved down the rail and lifted into the air. It flew for 12 seconds and went 120 feet (36.5 meters). But it flew. This was the beginning of the age of air travel.

Today, you can see the Wright Brothers' plane at the National Air and
45 Space Museum in Washington, D.C. And you can visit their Dayton bicycle shop in the Henry Ford Museum in Dearborn, Michigan.

Check Your Understanding

1. What did Wilbur Wright ask the U.S. Weather Bureau to send him?

___

___

2. In the ovals below, write three more words or phrases that describe the Wright Brothers, their personalities, or their actions. You do not have to use words from the reading.

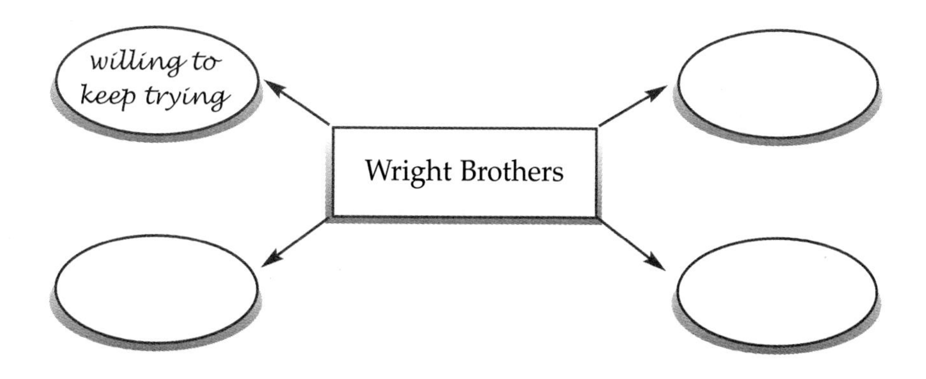

Build Your Vocabulary

What is the meaning of each word in red? Fill in the correct bubble.

1. A letter with a strange **request** arrived at the U.S. Weather Bureau in 1900. A bicycle maker in Dayton, Ohio, was asking for a list of windy places.

   Ⓐ unusual shape
   Ⓑ part of a bicycle
   Ⓒ statement about the weather
   Ⓓ act of asking for something

2. The brothers chose Kitty Hawk, North Carolina. It was an **isolated** area far from large towns.

   Ⓐ surrounded by water
   Ⓑ unexplored
   Ⓒ far away from other things
   Ⓓ mysterious

3. The wind blew the gliders in all directions. The pilots were helpless. Injuries and even **fatalities** were common.

   Ⓐ deaths
   Ⓑ storms
   Ⓒ accidents
   Ⓓ fires

4. The Wright Brothers thought they had a **solution** to the problem. By moving the wings and the tail, a pilot could control the plane.

   Ⓐ addition
   Ⓑ puzzle
   Ⓒ answer
   Ⓓ new fact

5. The Wright Brothers tried out more than 200 wings and tails on gliders until they found a **combination** that worked.

   Ⓐ powerful engine
   Ⓑ set of things that are used together
   Ⓒ book of carefully written plans
   Ⓓ something easy to build

6. Then they built an engine and **experimented** with propellers.

   Ⓐ flew
   Ⓑ tried different things
   Ⓒ played
   Ⓓ measured

Asking Yourself Questions

Asking yourself questions as you read is important. It helps you know what information you should look for and gives you ideas to discuss with other people. Possible question starters are *Who? What? Where? When? How? Why?* For example:

A letter with a strange request arrived at the U.S. Weather Bureau in 1900. A bicycle maker in Dayton, Ohio, was asking for a list of windy places. He also wanted the places to have lots of water or sand.

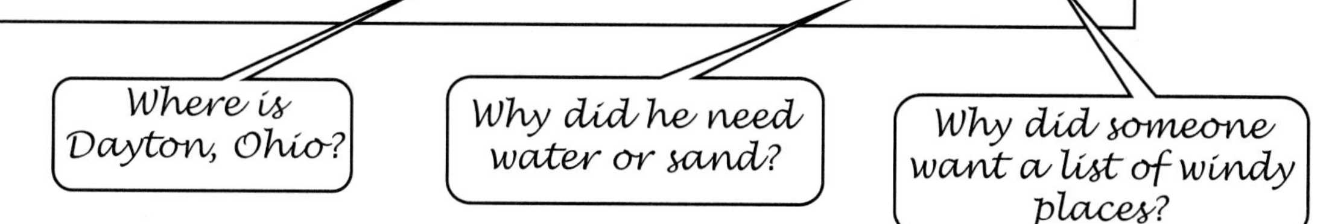

1. Read the paragraphs below. Ask yourself questions as you read and write your questions on the lines.

Questions

The Wright Brothers were not the first people to try to fly. Several inventors flew gliders without engines before, but they were never able to control the flight. The wind blew the gliders in all directions. The pilots were helpless. Injuries and even fatalities were common.

The Wright Brothers thought they had a solution to the problem. By moving the wings and the tail, a pilot could control the plane. The Wrights tried out more than 200 wings and tails on gliders until they found a combination that worked. Then they built an engine and experimented with propellers.

2. Meet in groups of two or three. Share your questions with your group and discuss possible answers.

Expand Your Vocabulary

Geometry

Read the definitions below of four words that are related to geometry, the study of lines and shapes.

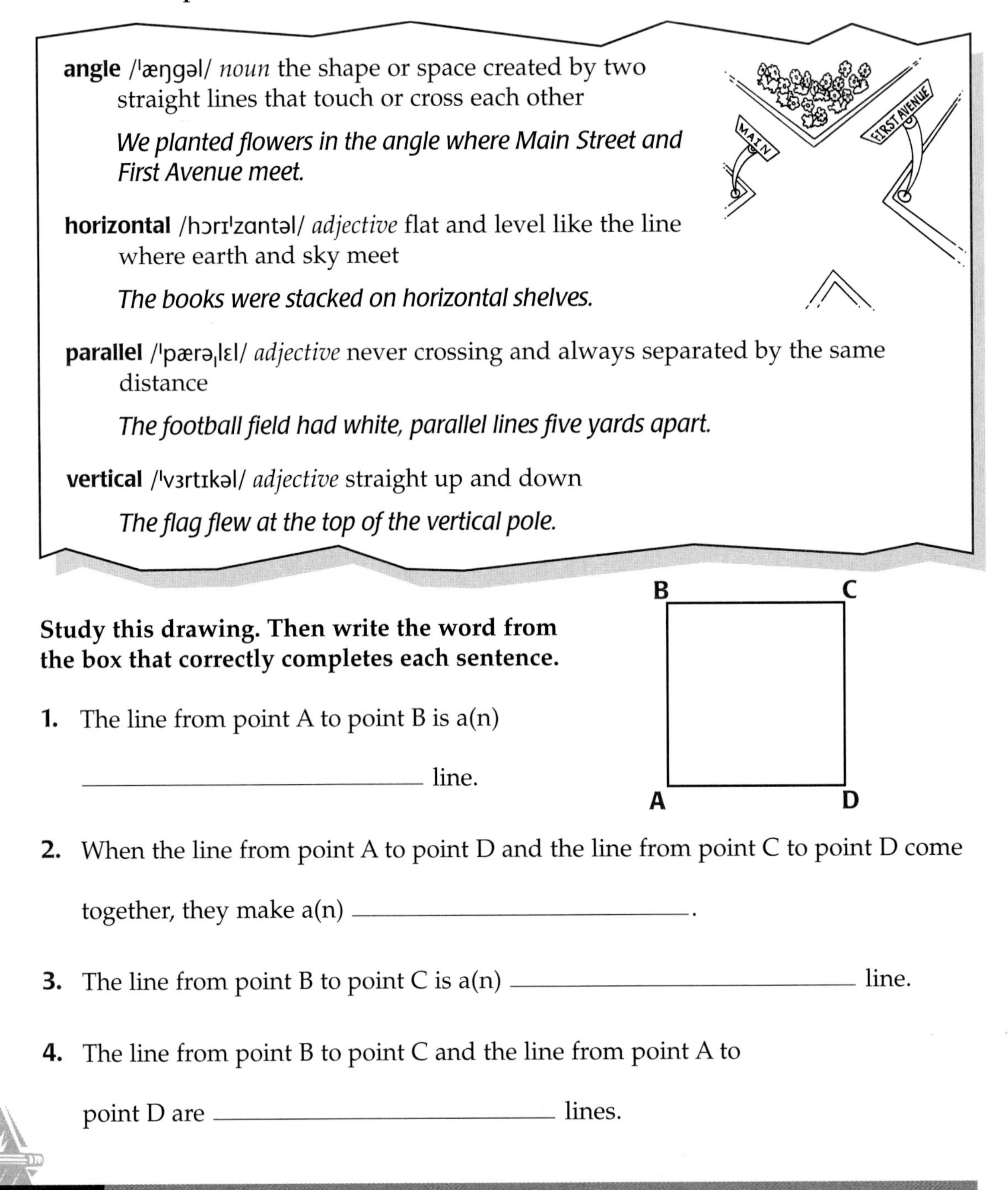

angle /ˈæŋgəl/ *noun* the shape or space created by two straight lines that touch or cross each other

We planted flowers in the angle where Main Street and First Avenue meet.

horizontal /hɔrɪˈzɑntəl/ *adjective* flat and level like the line where earth and sky meet

The books were stacked on horizontal shelves.

parallel /ˈpærəˌlɛl/ *adjective* never crossing and always separated by the same distance

The football field had white, parallel lines five yards apart.

vertical /ˈvɜrtɪkəl/ *adjective* straight up and down

The flag flew at the top of the vertical pole.

Study this drawing. Then write the word from the box that correctly completes each sentence.

1. The line from point A to point B is a(n) ______________________ line.

2. When the line from point A to point D and the line from point C to point D come together, they make a(n) ______________________.

3. The line from point B to point C is a(n) ______________________ line.

4. The line from point B to point C and the line from point A to point D are ______________________ lines.

Put It in Writing

Write a description of something you see in your classroom, such as the chalkboard, a desk, or a cabinet. Try to use one or more of the words above.

Number Prefixes

A *prefix* is a word part that is added to the beginning of a word or a root. (A *root* has meaning, but it is not always a word by itself.) The prefix changes the meaning of the word or the root. Some prefixes have meanings that have to do with numbers.

Prefix	Meaning	Example	Meaning
semi-	half or part	semicircle	half a circle
uni-	one	unicorn	animal with one horn
bi-	two	bicycle	cycle with two wheels
tri-	three	triangle	figure with three angles and three sides

Use the information above to answer each of these questions.

1. How many wheels are on a *unicycle*? ______________

2. How many numbers are used in a *binary* number system? ______________

3. How many months are in a *trimester?* ______________

4. How many times a year is a *semiannual* picnic held? ______________

5. If a store sends you a bill *bimonthly*, how many times must you pay each month? ______________

6. If you go to a sporting event called a *triathlon*, how many events do you expect to see? ______________

7. How many *universes* are there? ______________

8. If you *bisect* something, how many parts do you cut it into? ______________

- **Read the words in Column A and underline the number prefix in each word.**
- **Then circle any number words you see in Column B.**
- **Use these clues to help you as you choose the correct meanings. Next to each word on the left, write the letter for its meaning on the right. One has been done for you.**

	Column A	Column B
______	**1.** uniform	**a.** three people with the same mother who were born at the same time
______	**2.** trilogy	**b.** able to speak and write two languages
______	**3.** bilingual	**c.** having some but not all the ability needed for certain jobs
______	**4.** semifinal	**d.** a type of eyeglasses that has two different types of glass lenses
______	**5.** tripod	**e.** the same type of clothing worn by a group of people, such as workers or people in the army or navy
______	**6.** biweekly	**f.** a series of three books that tells one long story
a	**7.** triplets	**g.** an organization of workers formed in order to act and speak with one voice
______	**8.** bifocals	**h.** a game that comes just before the final game in a contest
______	**9.** union	**i.** happening every two weeks or twice a week
______	**10.** semiskilled	**j.** a stand held up by three legs

Now check your answers in a dictionary.

People on a hill in San Francisco, California, watch the fires after the 1906 earthquake.

CHAPTER

The San Francisco Earthquake

Reading Skill: Visualizing

Expand Your Vocabulary: Earthquakes

Get Ready to Read

1. Imagine that you are in a very bad earthquake. How will you feel? Where will you go? What will you do?

____

____

2. Look at the picture above. List three things that you think were changed by the earthquake. Form groups of two or three and share your answers.

____

____

The San Francisco Earthquake

San Francisco after the earthquake

The earthquake lasted less than a minute. But it destroyed over 28,000 buildings, knocked down 490 city blocks, made 250,000 people homeless, and killed more than 3,000 people. At the time, people **estimated** the total damage to be $500,000. No one can be sure. Today it would cost billions of dollars to fix that much damage.

The worst natural **disaster** in American history began at 5:12 A.M., April 18, 1906, in San Francisco, California.* First, small earth **tremors** shook dishes and windows. Seconds later, people felt the full power of the earthquake. Violent movements of the earth threw people out of bed. They tried hard to stand as the floors under them moved back and forth and rolled up and down. Dishes flew across the room. Tables and pianos bounced around like toys. Lights swung back and forth from ceilings and then crashed to the floor. When people understood what was happening, they ran into the street. Bricks fell from buildings and killed many people as they stepped outside.

Finally, the shaking stopped. People stood together in the streets and saw a changed city. Entire blocks of buildings were gone. The buildings that were still there were badly damaged. The tracks for the city's streetcars were twisted and unusable. Broken water pipes shot water into the air. Most frightening of all, however, were the fires that were burning everywhere.

Bricks, electrical wires, and other objects in the streets kept ambulances from reaching injured people. There was no water to fight the fires, and many firemen lay dying in the **ruins** of their fire stations.

As night began, people were too afraid to return home even if their houses were still there. The night sky was bright from the light of the fires all over the city. To keep the fires from spreading, some remaining buildings were blown up.

* See the map on the inside back cover for the location of San Francisco in the United States.

35 When news of the disaster reached people outside of San Francisco, they sent food, water, tents, and medicine. On April 23, five days after the earthquake, the governor of California announced that the people of San Francisco were already beginning to rebuild the city. But the great earthquake taught the builders important lessons.

40 Today California has more than a thousand very **sensitive** instruments that report even very small earth movements. Computers can **predict** where and when earthquakes are most likely to happen. Buildings and bridges are built to remain standing in an earthquake. Earthquakes are still a danger, but the city of San Francisco is better prepared now than it was in 1906.

San Francisco today

Check Your Understanding

1. Why were ambulances unable to reach injured people?

____

____

2. Why were people afraid to return to their homes after the earthquake was over?

____

____

3. Why were some buildings blown up?

____

____

Build Your Vocabulary

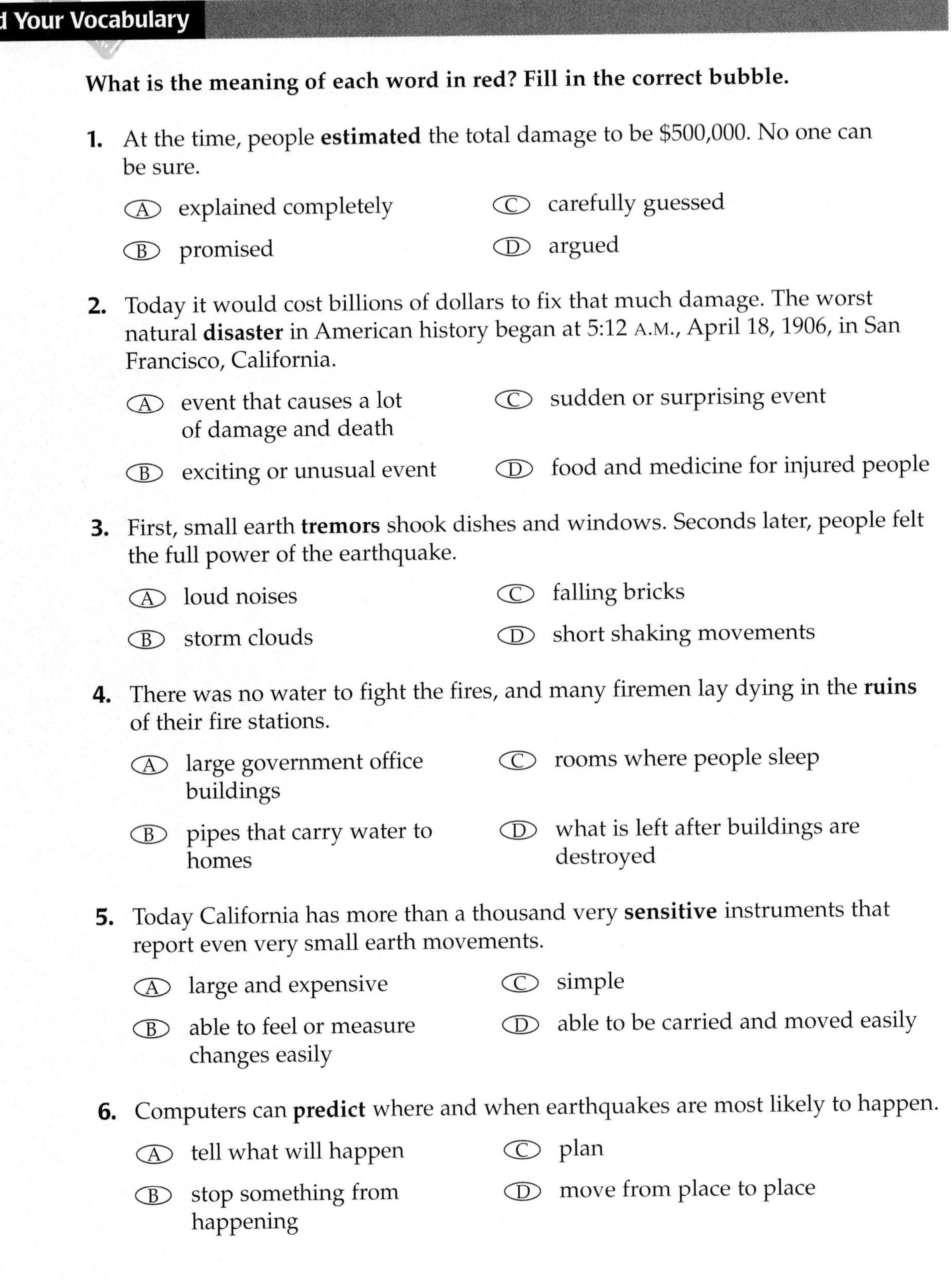

What is the meaning of each word in red? Fill in the correct bubble.

1. At the time, people **estimated** the total damage to be $500,000. No one can be sure.

   Ⓐ explained completely
   Ⓑ promised
   Ⓒ carefully guessed
   Ⓓ argued

2. Today it would cost billions of dollars to fix that much damage. The worst natural **disaster** in American history began at 5:12 A.M., April 18, 1906, in San Francisco, California.

   Ⓐ event that causes a lot of damage and death
   Ⓑ exciting or unusual event
   Ⓒ sudden or surprising event
   Ⓓ food and medicine for injured people

3. First, small earth **tremors** shook dishes and windows. Seconds later, people felt the full power of the earthquake.

   Ⓐ loud noises
   Ⓑ storm clouds
   Ⓒ falling bricks
   Ⓓ short shaking movements

4. There was no water to fight the fires, and many firemen lay dying in the **ruins** of their fire stations.

   Ⓐ large government office buildings
   Ⓑ pipes that carry water to homes
   Ⓒ rooms where people sleep
   Ⓓ what is left after buildings are destroyed

5. Today California has more than a thousand very **sensitive** instruments that report even very small earth movements.

   Ⓐ large and expensive
   Ⓑ able to feel or measure changes easily
   Ⓒ simple
   Ⓓ able to be carried and moved easily

6. Computers can **predict** where and when earthquakes are most likely to happen.

   Ⓐ tell what will happen
   Ⓑ stop something from happening
   Ⓒ plan
   Ⓓ move from place to place

Visualizing

When you read, it is helpful to make pictures in your mind. Try to "see" the people, things, or events the writer is describing. This is called *visualizing*.

1. Reread these sentences from the reading selection. As you read, visualize what is happening.

> Violent movements of the earth threw people out of bed. They tried hard to stand as the floors under them moved back and forth and rolled up and down. Dishes flew across the room. Tables and pianos bounced around like toys. Lights swung back and forth from ceilings and then crashed to the floor.

2. Draw a picture on your own paper showing how you visualize the event the writer describes. Write a title for your picture.

3. Reread this paragraph from the reading selection. Visualize the scene.

> Finally, the shaking stopped. People stood together in the streets and saw a changed city. Entire blocks of buildings were gone. The buildings that were still there were badly damaged. The tracks for the city's streetcars were twisted and unusable. Broken water pipes shot water into the air. Most frightening of all, however, were the fires that were burning everywhere.

4. Draw a picture showing how you visualize the scene. Share your picture with a partner and discuss what you drew.

5. Reread the reading selection on pages 16 and 17. Visualize the people, things, and events as you read.

Expand Your Vocabulary

Earthquakes

Read the definitions below of four words that are related to earthquakes.

fault /fɔlt/ *noun* a large crack in the Earth's surface

Scientists predict a large earthquake along the San Andreas Fault.

geology /dʒiˈɑlədʒi/ *noun* the scientific study of the Earth and the rocks and soil it is made of

Because of geology, we are learning more about earthquakes.

magnitude /ˈmægnəˌtud/ *noun* how powerful an earthquake is

The earthquake's magnitude was small, and there was not much damage.

Richter Scale /ˈrɪktər ˌskeɪl/ *noun* a system for measuring the size of an earthquake

The earthquake measured six on the Richter Scale.

Fill in each blank with the correct word from above.

1. I don't know the ______________________ of the earthquake, but it felt very big.

2. We are studying ______________________ and learning about different kinds of rocks.

3. People who live near a ______________________ are sometimes worried about an earthquake.

4. Some people may not feel an earthquake that measures one or two on the ______________________.

Put It in Writing

Write a short newspaper story about the San Francisco earthquake or another earthquake. Try to use one or more of the words above.

CHAPTER

Women in New York demand the right to vote in the early 1900s.

Women Win the Right to Vote

Reading Skill:
Using Context Clues

Expand Your Vocabulary:
The Right to Vote

Get Ready to Read

1. Imagine there is a law in your town or city that you feel is unfair. What are some things you might do to get the law changed?

___

___

___

2. Look at the women in the picture above and read the title of this chapter. What do you think you will learn about American history in this essay?

___

___

___

Women Win the Right to Vote

In 1776, men were in charge of things. They held most jobs and ran the government. People thought that a woman's place was in the home. It is not surprising then that the Declaration of Independence, which was written in 1776, says, "all *men* are created equal." So for 144 years, only men had the right to vote in nearly every state. It took a long, hard fight to change that.

The fight began in 1848 when some women met in Seneca Falls, New York. There they decided to try to get "suffrage," or the right to vote. Susan B. Anthony and Elizabeth Cady Stanton led the group. The women knew they needed to change the U.S. Constitution, the basic rules of the government. This is not easy to do. First, two-thirds of both parts of Congress, the Senate and the House of Representatives, must approve the change. Then, three-fourths of all the state governments must also approve it.

Anthony and Stanton spoke at large meetings and organized **protests** and parades. The women carried signs that said the voting laws were unfair. They wanted the men in government to listen to their **demands** and agree to change the Constitution. Many people made fun of these women and even attacked them. When Anthony broke a New York law by voting, she was arrested.

Finally, in 1868, a change to the Constitution was formally presented in Congress. This **amendment** was going to give women the right to vote. But the men in Congress refused to vote on it. This **process** was repeated every year until 1887. Then Congress did vote on this change and the amendment was easily **defeated**. The fight seemed over.

However, in 1913, new leaders in the Women's Suffrage Movement asked their members to start having protests and parades again. Five thousand women held a **rally** in Washington, D.C. After many men went to fight in World War I, women did their jobs while they were away. People began to ask why women who were doing men's jobs could not vote. This seemed very unfair.

Women do men's jobs during World War I.

Finally, in 1918, Congress passed the Nineteenth Amendment. It said that no one could be stopped from voting because of his or her sex. Two years later, it was passed by 36 of the 48 states. It was now part of the Constitution.

Six months before the Nineteenth Amendment passed, the National American Woman Suffrage Association held a big meeting. At this meeting the League of Women Voters was formed. Its goal is to get everyone to take part in government. This organization is still helping to educate American voters today.

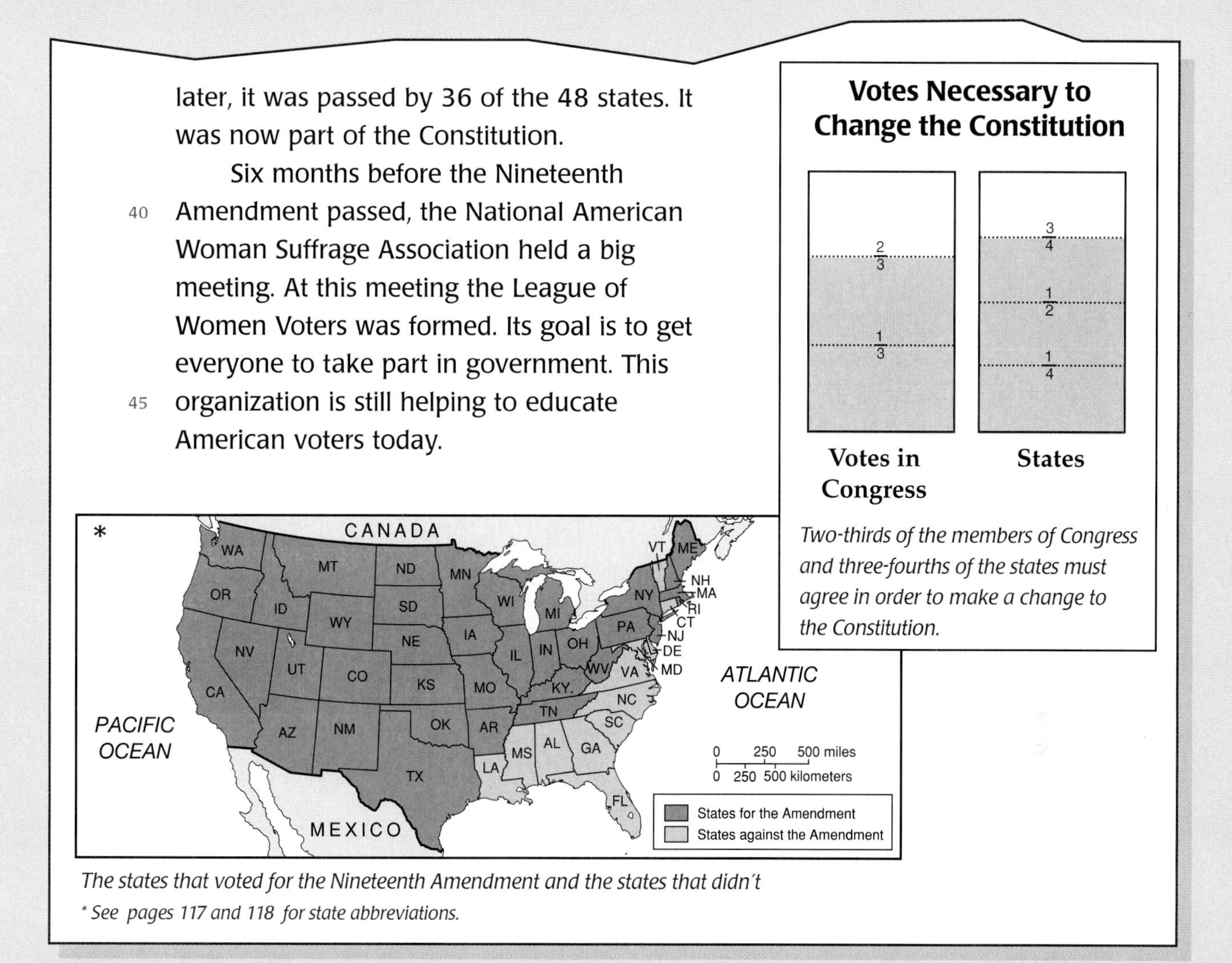

Two-thirds of the members of Congress and three-fourths of the states must agree in order to make a change to the Constitution.

The states that voted for the Nineteenth Amendment and the states that didn't

** See pages 117 and 118 for state abbreviations.*

Check Your Understanding

1. How can the U.S. Constitution be changed?

____

____

____

2. Why was Susan B. Anthony arrested in New York?

____

____

3. How did World War I help women win the right to vote?

____

____

Build Your Vocabulary

What is the meaning of each word in red? Fill in the correct bubble.

1. Anthony and Stanton spoke at large meetings and organized **protests** and parades. The women carried signs that said the voting laws were unfair.

   Ⓐ old or unfair laws that need to be changed
   Ⓑ religious meetings
   Ⓒ actions that show that people don't like something
   Ⓓ requests for money

2. They wanted the men in government to listen to their **demands** and agree to change the Constitution.

   Ⓐ strong requests
   Ⓑ songs and speeches
   Ⓒ leaders of a large group
   Ⓓ interesting stories

3. Finally, in 1868, a change to the Constitution was formally presented in Congress. This **amendment** was going to give women the right to vote.

   Ⓐ disagreement
   Ⓑ presentation
   Ⓒ repair
   Ⓓ change

4. Finally, in 1868, a change to the Constitution was formerly presented in Congress. This amendment was going to give women the right to vote. But the men in Congress refused to vote on it. This **process** was repeated every year until 1887.

   Ⓐ series of actions or events
   Ⓑ wish to vote
   Ⓒ loud argument
   Ⓓ government problem

5. Then Congress did vote on this change and the amendment was easily **defeated**. The fight seemed over.

   Ⓐ made into a law
   Ⓑ beaten in a vote or fight
   Ⓒ hidden
   Ⓓ sent back

6. However, in 1913, new leaders in the Women's Suffrage Movement asked their members to start having protests and parades again. Five thousand women held a **rally** in Washington, D.C.

   Ⓐ vote to choose new leaders of an organization
   Ⓑ large public meeting to show that people like an idea
   Ⓒ quiet march around a particular building such as the Capitol
   Ⓓ illegal meeting

Using Context Clues

When you don't know a word in a reading selection, use the words and sentences before and after it to help you guess its meaning. These words and sentences are called context clues. For example:

> Anthony and Stanton spoke at large meetings and organized **protests** and parades. The women carried signs that said the voting laws were unfair.

The women carried signs that showed they didn't like the voting laws. A *protest*, therefore, is probably about showing that people don't like something.

Look at these sentences from the reading selection again. Underline the words or sentences that help you guess the meaning of the words in red.

1. They wanted the men in government to listen to their **demands** and agree to change the Constitution.

2. Finally, in 1868, a change to the Constitution was formally presented in Congress. This **amendment** was going to give women the right to vote.

3. Finally, in 1868, a change to the Constitution was formally presented in Congress. This amendment was going to give women the right to vote. But the men in Congress refused to vote on it. This **process** was repeated every year until 1887.

4. Then Congress did vote on this change and the amendment was easily **defeated**. The fight seemed over.

5. However, in 1913, new leaders in the Women's Suffrage Movement asked their members to start having protests and parades again. Five thousand women held a **rally** in Washington, D.C.

Now look again at your answers to the vocabulary questions on page 24. Change any answers you think are wrong.

Expand Your Vocabulary

The Right to Vote

Read the definitions below of four words that are related to voting.

campaign /kæmˈpeɪn/ *noun* a series of actions done by a person or group of people to reach a goal, such as winning an election

Many young people worked in the senator's campaign for re-election.

candidate /ˈkændɪdˌdeɪt/ *noun* a person who is trying to be elected to a government job

The candidate for the Senate agreed to answer the reporters' questions.

majority /məˈdʒɔrəti/ *noun* (plural **majorities**) more than half

To win an election, a candidate needs to get a majority of the votes.

primary election /ˌpraɪmɛri ɪˈlɛkʃən/ *noun* an early election in which voters choose a small number of people to compete in a later election

The primary election was held eight weeks before the general election.

Write the correct word from above next to each clue.

____________________ **1.** People who want to be elected for the same job may have to compete in one of these.

____________________ **2.** This is what one of the people who compete in an election is called.

____________________ **3.** If there are 100 votes in an election, 51 votes is this.

____________________ **4.** Someone who wants to be elected will need money for this.

Put It in Writing

Write a letter to a newspaper that tells why you think voting is important. Try to use one or more of the words above.

Reading Comprehension Tests

Some tests ask you to read a passage and answer questions about it. Sometimes the answers to the questions are not stated directly. However, you can use the facts that are stated to guess certain facts that are not stated. This is called making *inferences*.

Practice this strategy on the sample reading selection and questions below.

Directions: Read the selection below. Choose the best answer to the questions.

The battle to gain a woman's right to vote began in 1848. However, many women who met in Seneca Falls that year thought that demanding the vote was asking too much. They just wanted jobs and an education. At that time, a woman's life usually involved only marriage and family. But after the Civil War, gaining the right to vote became important to more women. Then the Fifteenth Amendment to the Constitution was passed. This amendment gave African American men the right to vote. Disagreements over this amendment weakened women's efforts to gain the vote. Some women were against this amendment because it did not include women. Other women supported it and thought it would lead to women getting the vote.

Sample Questions

S1. You can tell from this passage that—

- Ⓐ few women attended the meeting in Seneca Falls.
- Ⓑ women were very helpful during the Civil War.
- Ⓒ in 1848 most women married and raised families.
- Ⓓ the Fifteenth Amendment passed easily.

S2. After the Civil War,—

- Ⓐ most African-American men did not want women to have the right to vote.
- Ⓑ most women decided to give up trying to get the vote.
- Ⓒ the Fifteenth Amendment helped women get the vote.
- Ⓓ women worked even hardeer to get the right to vote.

If women's lives involved only marriage and family, you should be able to guess that most women married and raised families, so the answer to S1 is C. Did you use the stated facts to guess the answer to S2? The correct answer is on page 122.

Go on

PRACTICE TEST

Directions: Read the selection below. Choose the BEST answer to each question.

In 1918, Congress passed the Nineteenth Amendment. This gave women the right to vote. Before it could become a law, however, the governments of 36 states had to approve it. Wisconsin and Illinois rushed to be the first to approve the amendment. Georgia and Alabama rushed just as quickly to reject it. The vote in other states was uncertain. The arguments for and against the amendment went on and on. When one side thought it was going to lose, it found a way to delay the vote. Nevertheless, by 1920, 35 states had approved the amendment. Just one more state was needed. Tennessee was the only state that still planned to vote. The vote was sure to be close. People in favor of the amendment and those against it rushed to Tennessee. It appeared that the amendment was going to be defeated. Then at the last moment, a young lawmaker changed his vote because his mother told him to. The amendment passed, and the Nineteenth Amendment became law.

1. Wisconsin and Illinois —

- (A) gave women the right to vote before 1918.
- (B) were proud to approve the amendment.
- (C) wanted to make Alabama and Georgia look foolish.
- (D) needed more women workers.

2. When one side thought it would lose, it tried to delay the vote —

- (A) so it could try to change the minds of some voters.
- (B) because other states were changing their votes.
- (C) because an amendment becomes law unless states vote against it.
- (D) in order to make lawmakers tired and want to go home.

3. People for and against the amendment went to Tennessee —

- (A) to stop the vote.
- (B) to count the votes.
- (C) because it was between Wisconsin and Georgia.
- (D) to work for their side.

4. The mother of the young Tennessee lawmaker told him —

- (A) to vote for the amendment.
- (B) to vote against the amendment.
- (C) not to vote on the amendment.
- (D) to delay the vote on the amendment.

Correct answers are on page 122.

STOP

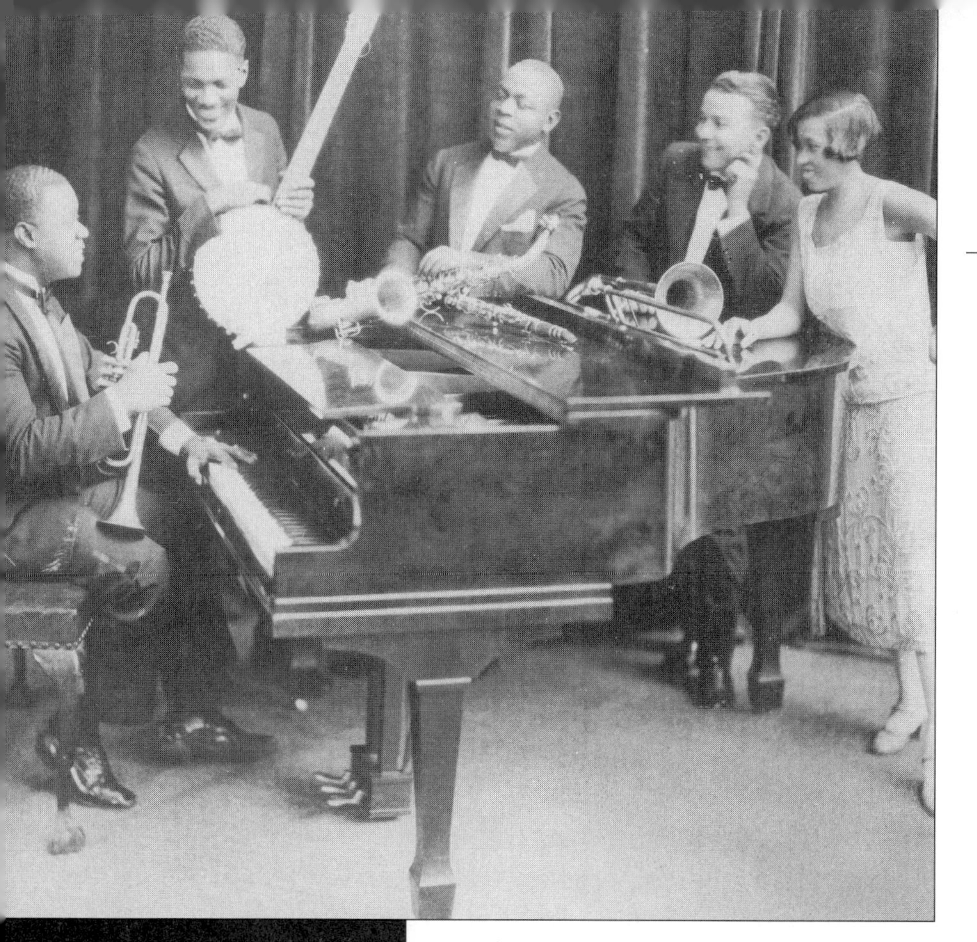

African-American jazz musicians in the 1920s

CHAPTER

The Jazz Age

Reading Skill:
Noticing Cause and Effect

Expand Your Vocabulary:
Music

Get Ready to Read

1. List some things nearly everyone does today that probably shocked some people 90 years ago. Form groups of two or three and share your answers.

____

____

____

2. Look at the picture above and read the title of the chapter. What do you think the Jazz Age was like? Why do you think it has that name?

____

____

____

The Jazz Age

In the 1920s, young people in the United States seemed to be having a wild party. A few years earlier, many Americans died in World War I. Then a serious illness, influenza, spread across the country. This **epidemic** killed thousands more people. But in the 1920s, Americans were beginning to enjoy life again. Cars and home **appliances** such as toasters and washing machines were making life easier. People had money to spend. Women began to change the way they dressed, behaved, and had fun. Parents were shocked when their daughters cut their hair short, put on makeup, and wore clothes that showed their knees and arms. Young women even started smoking. And young people everywhere were doing wild new dances.

In the South, African Americans were creating a new kind of music called jazz. It combined work songs, religious music, and African beats. Unlike with other music, musical notes for jazz were not written down, and jazz songs were played differently every time. Jazz, therefore, was always new, fresh, and exciting. Most homes had radios, so people heard jazz everywhere.

The Eighteenth Amendment to the Constitution passed on January 16, 1920. This amendment **prohibited** making, selling, and transporting alcohol. No law in U.S. history was so often disobeyed. People still wanted their alcohol, and criminal organizations were happy to sell it to them. Secret nightclubs called speakeasies opened everywhere. People said a secret password to enter. Inside they got drinks, a show, and lots of jazz.

Criminal organizations earned millions of dollars by selling illegal alcohol. During the 1920s, large criminal organizations existed in Chicago, Illinois. Men like Al Capone and George "Bugs" Moran were their leaders. They fought violently to control the illegal business. Men were murdered, and businesses were blown up.

Al Capone is arrested.

35 On the positive side, during the Jazz Age there were many **remarkable** people in America. Charles Lindbergh made the first nonstop flight from New York City to Paris, France. African-American writers and poets like Langston Hughes wrote about their history. Babe Ruth, the New York Yankees star baseball player, hit a record 60 home runs. Georgia
40 O'Keeffe painted beautiful pictures of flowers and animal bones.

But when the 1920s ended, the party stopped. The sale of alcohol became legal again, so the speakeasies closed. Capone was in Alcatraz, a prison in San Francisco Bay. People lost their money when stock prices suddenly fell, banks closed, and businesses went **bankrupt**. One thing did
45 not end. Jazz lived on. Today jazz remains a **unique** American form of music. It is popular all over the world.

Check Your Understanding

1. How did jazz differ from other kinds of music?

____

____

____

2. Why was a secret password needed to enter a speakeasy?

____

____

____

3. Name three famous people from the Jazz Age. Why were they famous?

____

____

____

Build Your Vocabulary

What is the meaning of each word in red? Fill in the correct bubble.

1. Then a serious illness, influenza, spread across the country. This **epidemic** killed thousands more people.

   (A) disease that spreads quickly
   (B) war between powerful countries
   (C) mysterious injuries
   (D) place where sick people are taken

2. Cars and home **appliances** such as toasters and washing machines were making life easier.

   (A) family trips
   (B) things that soldiers brought home after World War I
   (C) songs and dances
   (D) small machines that do work in the house

3. This amendment **prohibited** making, selling, and transporting alcohol. No law in U.S. history was so often disobeyed. People still wanted their alcohol, and criminal organizations were happy to sell it to them.

   (A) made something illegal
   (B) allowed something
   (C) asked people to do something
   (D) increased the cost of something

4. On the positive side, during the Jazz Age there were many **remarkable** people in America. Charles Lindbergh made the first nonstop flight from New York City to Paris, France.

   (A) unknown
   (B) unusual and great
   (C) foolish
   (D) wise

5. People lost their money when stock prices suddenly fell, banks closed, and businesses went **bankrupt**.

   (A) sold for a lot of money
   (B) unable to pay what they owed and to continue doing business
   (C) likely to ask banks to lend them money
   (D) able to invent new things to make and sell

6. Today jazz remains a **unique** American form of music. It is popular all over the world.

   (A) difficult
   (B) old-fashioned
   (C) different from anything else
   (D) surprising

Noticing Cause and Effect

A *cause* is the reason something happens. An *effect* is the thing that happens.

Cause: A serious illness spread across the country.

Effect: It killed thousands more people.

Words such as *as a result, because, for that reason, so,* and *therefore* signal a cause and an effect.

Read the reading selection again and look for causes and effects. Write the missing causes and effects in the chart below. The first one has been done for you.

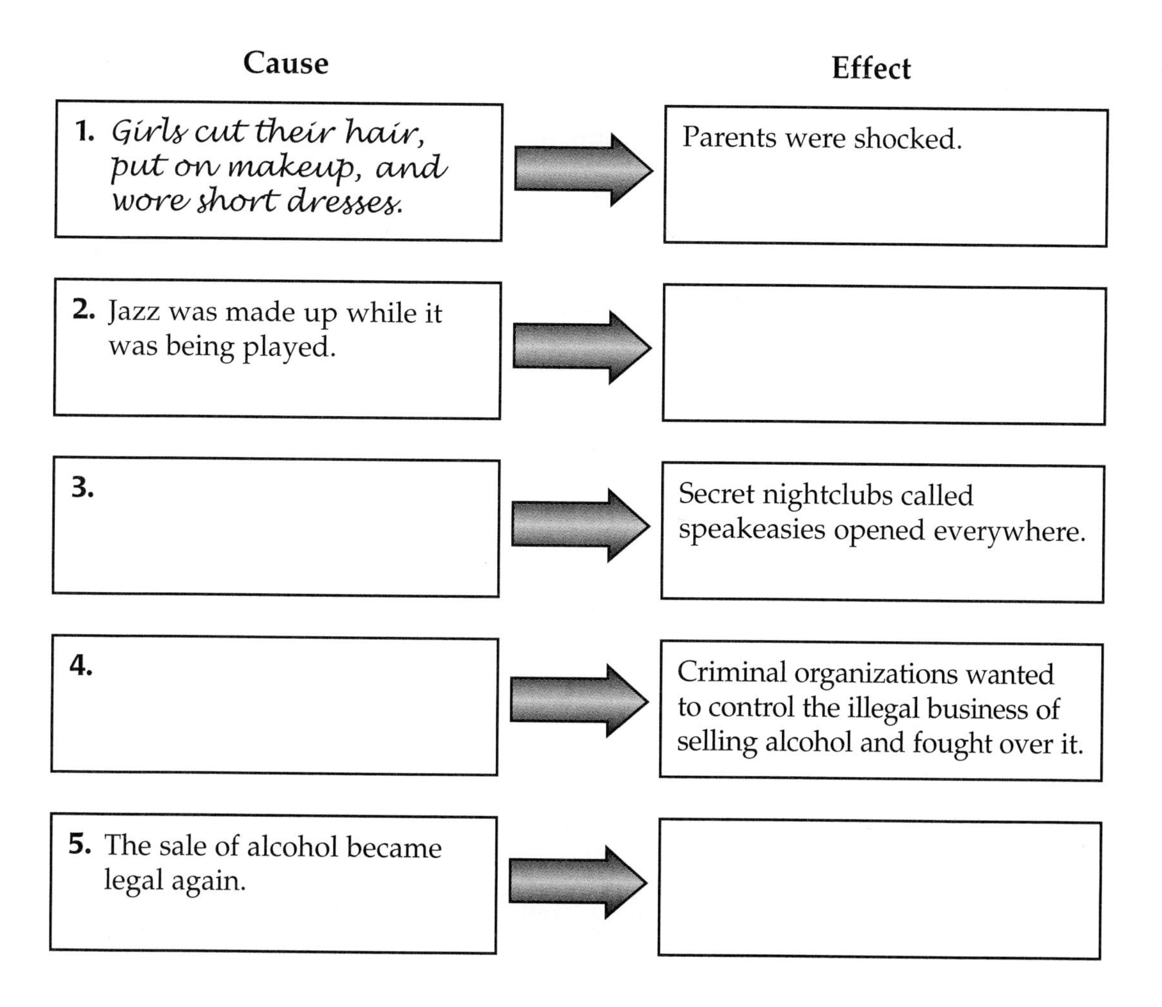

Cause		Effect
1. *Girls cut their hair, put on makeup, and wore short dresses.*	→	Parents were shocked.
2. Jazz was made up while it was being played.	→	
3.	→	Secret nightclubs called speakeasies opened everywhere.
4.	→	Criminal organizations wanted to control the illegal business of selling alcohol and fought over it.
5. The sale of alcohol became legal again.	→	

Expand Your Vocabulary

Music

Read the definitions below of four words that are related to music.

harmony /ˈhɑrməni/ *noun* a pleasant combination of two or more musical sounds

The two singers sang several songs in perfect harmony.

rhythm /ˈrɪðəm/ *noun* a pattern of repeated notes or beats in music

People tapped their feet to the rhythm of the music.

solo /ˈsoʊloʊ/ *noun* (plural **solos**) one voice or musical instrument performing music alone

The concert included a solo by the lead guitarist.

trio /ˈtrioʊ/ *noun* (plural **trios**) a group of three people or instruments performing music

The trio was made up of a piano, drums, and guitar.

True or False? Use the definitions. Fill in the correct bubble.

	True	False
1. Musicians never want to make harmony.	(T)	(F)
2. One musical instrument can be used for a solo.	(T)	(F)
3. A trio can create harmony.	(T)	(F)
4. You can clap your hands to the rhythm of a song.	(T)	(F)
5. A trio can sing a solo.	(T)	(F)

Put It in Writing

Write a paragraph about a kind of music you like but older people often think is strange or unusual. Tell why you like it. Try to use one or more of the words above.

Dorothea Lange takes photographs from the roof of her car.

CHAPTER

Dorothea Lange: Photographer of the Great Depression

Reading Skill:
Separating Facts from Opinions

Expand Your Vocabulary:
Money and Banking

Get Ready to Read

1. You want to tell a friend living far away about your town or community. Will you describe it in a letter or email or send pictures? Explain your answer.

    ____

2. Read the title of this chapter and look at the pictures on this page and the next two pages. What do you think the Great Depression was? When and where did it happen?

    ____

Dorothea Lange: Photographer of the Great Depression

The good times of the Jazz Age ended on October 29, 1929, a day called Black Tuesday. On that day, many businesses suddenly became worth a lot less money. People who owned parts of these businesses lost their money. Workers all over the country lost their jobs. Without money, people could not repay loans. As a result, banks didn't have money for people who wanted their savings. Some families lost their homes and lived in tents. Others moved from place to place looking for work. The years of **prosperity** came to an end. It was the start of the Great Depression.

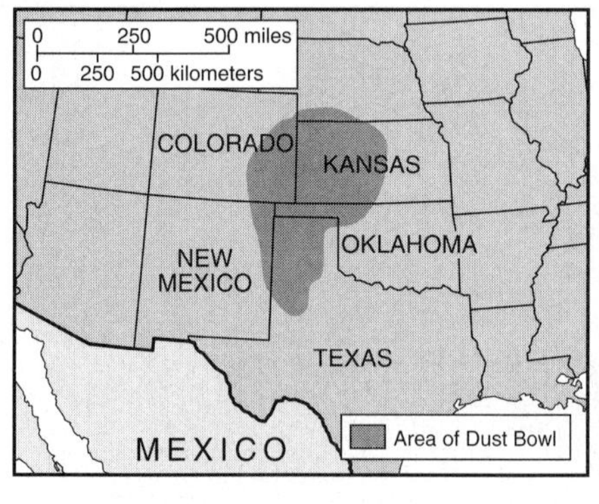

The Dust Bowl affected a large area of the United States.

On many farms, things were even worse. Earlier, farmers plowed away the grass and trees that held the soil. Then it didn't rain for several years. Now dry winds blew the loose dirt away. Dark dust filled the skies. Only **unproductive** land that could not grow crops was left. Parts of Kansas, Oklahoma, Texas, Colorado, and New Mexico became known as the Dust Bowl.

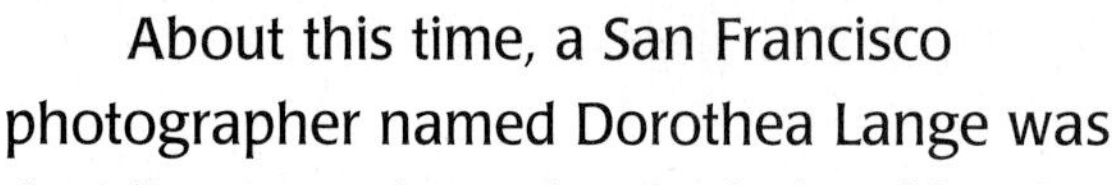

About this time, a San Francisco photographer named Dorothea Lange was deciding to make a change in her life. She took pictures of people in her studio. Her business was successful, but she was bored. So in 1929, Lange decided to leave her studio and take her camera into the streets. She wanted to take pictures of people as they really were.

White Angel Breadline, *San Francisco, California, 1933*

Lange first got to know the people she wanted to photograph. She asked about their families and their **backgrounds**. In this way, she got them to trust her and let her take their pictures. But she did not ask them to stand or sit in **artificial** ways. She waited until the people were acting natural. Then she took their pictures. She took shocking pictures of

desperate men begging for jobs or standing in long lines to get a cup of soup. Her photographs told the story of the Great Depression better than words could.

40 The government hired Lange to report on the living conditions of families from the Dust Bowl. During this time she took her most famous photograph, *Migrant Mother*. It is a picture of a tired mother and her starving 45 children on a farm. The mother's face shows a mixture of worry and **determination**, the strength to go on. This picture appeared in many newspapers and caused the government to send 20,000 pounds of food to her farm.

50 Lange did not think of herself as an artist. Even so, three months after her death in 1965, her photographs were shown at the Museum of Modern Art in New York. Today her photographs are in the Oakland Museum of California.

Migrant Mother, *Nipomo, California, 1936*

Check Your Understanding

1. Why did farmlands turn to dust and blow away in 1929?

____

____

____

2. Why did Dorothea Lange get to know the people before she photographed them?

____

____

____

3. The reading selection says that Lange's photographs tell a story. What story does the photograph called *White Angel Breadline* tell?

____

____

____

Build Your Vocabulary

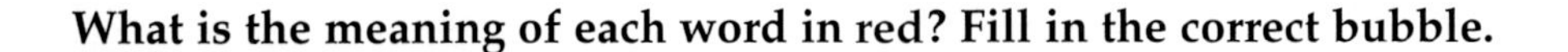

What is the meaning of each word in red? Fill in the correct bubble.

1. Some families lost their homes and lived in tents. Others moved from place to place looking for work. The years of **prosperity** came to an end.

   Ⓐ anger and hate
   Ⓑ poverty and hunger
   Ⓒ success and money
   Ⓓ crime

2. Now dry winds blew the loose dirt away. Dark dust filled the skies. Only **unproductive** land that could not grow crops was left.

   Ⓐ beautiful
   Ⓑ easy to sell
   Ⓒ dangerous
   Ⓓ unable to bring good results

3. Lange first got to know the people she wanted to photograph. She asked about their families and their **backgrounds**. In this way, she got them to trust her and let her take their pictures.

   Ⓐ past and present life
   Ⓑ amount of money in banks
   Ⓒ favorite foods
   Ⓓ knowledge of photography

4. But she did not ask them to stand or sit in some **artificial** way. She waited until the people were acting natural.

   Ⓐ unnatural
   Ⓑ exciting
   Ⓒ stupid
   Ⓓ loud

5. She took shocking pictures of **desperate** men begging for jobs or standing in long lines to get a cup of soup.

   Ⓐ strong and active
   Ⓑ needing something badly
   Ⓒ strange or unusual
   Ⓓ old

6. The mother's face shows a mixture of worry and **determination,** the strength to go on.

   Ⓐ hopelessness about the future
   Ⓑ hunger
   Ⓒ happiness
   Ⓓ strong desire to continue trying

Separating Facts from Opinions

A *fact* is something that you can prove. An *opinion* is someone's idea or belief that cannot be proved. You can agree or disagree with an opinion. Opinions often use words such as *good, bad, best, worst,* and *too.*

Fact: October 29, 1929, is called Black Tuesday.

Opinion: Black Tuesday is the worst day in U.S. history.

Fact or Opinion? Fill in the correct bubble.

	Fact	Opinion
1. Some people lost their homes during the Great Depression.	(F)	(O)
2. Farmers plowed away the grass and trees.	(F)	(O)
3. Too many people lived on farms in 1929.	(F)	(O)
4. Taking people's photographs in a studio is boring work.	(F)	(O)
5. Dorothea Lange made a change in her life in 1929.	(F)	(O)
6. *Migrant Mother* is Dorothea Lange's best photograph.	(F)	(O)
7. The government hired Lange to do a report.	(F)	(O)
8. The government waited too long to send food to starving families.	(F)	(O)
9. Lange's photographs were shown at the Museum of Modern Art.	(F)	(O)
10. Lange is a great artist.	(F)	(O)

Expand Your Vocabulary

Money and Banking

Read the definitions below of four words that are related to money and banking.

deposit /dɪˈpɑzɪt/ *verb* to put money in a bank

I always deposit part of my pay in a savings account.

inflation /ɪnˈfleɪʃən/ *noun* the continuing rise of prices over time

Last year inflation caused the price of everything to go up five percent.

interest /ˈɪntrəst/ *noun* money you pay to borrow money, or money a bank pays you for saving your money there

This bank charges less interest on loans than the one across the street.

withdraw /wɪθˈdrɔ/ *verb* to take money out of a bank account

She withdraws money from her savings account to pay the bills.

Fill in each blank with the correct word from above.

This year I will **(1)**____________________ $10 into my savings account every month. I am saving the money to buy a bike. When I **(2)**____________________ the money at the end of the year, I will have $123. This is more than I will put into the account. That is because the bank pays me **(3)**____________________ on the money I save. I will then have enough money for the bike unless **(4)**____________________ makes its price go up.

Put It in Writing

Write a paragraph. Tell about how you earned some money and what you did with it. It can be a real story, or you can make it up. Try to use one or more of the words above.

Suffixes

A *suffix* is a word part that is added to the end of a word. The suffix changes how the word is used. The suffixes **–tion** or **–ion** and **–ment** change *verbs* (action words) into *nouns* (naming words). Drop the *e* at the end of a word when you add *–ion*.

verb	+	suffix	=	noun
suggest	+	-ion	=	suggestion
produce	+	-tion	=	production
treat	+	-ment	=	treatment

Add one of the suffixes above to the underlined verb in the first of each pair of sentences. Then write the noun you've made on the line to complete the second sentence. In sentences marked with an asterisk (*), drop the final –*e* before you add the suffix.

*1. The teachers worked hard to educate the students.

All the students got a good ______________________.

2. The dancers move gracefully over the stage.

The audience watches their ______________________ very closely.

3. Theresa wanted to connect her computer to the Internet.

She was able to make the ______________________ easily.

4. We hope to achieve the goal of collecting $5,000.

If we do it, it will be a great ______________________.

5. Tomorrow we will discuss the reading.

I hope it will be an interesting ______________________.

6. Our teachers usually assign homework for us to do.

Tonight I have only one ______________________ to finish.

*7. If we all cooperate, we will finish the job quickly.

Your ______________________ will be very helpful.

8. A rock band will entertain us at the dance.

This ______________________ will not make everybody happy.

You can use the suffix **–able** to change *verbs* into *adjectives* (describing words). This suffix means "able to be done." You can use the suffix **–ous** to change *nouns* or *verbs* into *adjectives*. This suffix means "full of something." You often drop the *e* at the end of a word when you add these suffixes.

verb/noun	+	suffix	=	adjective	meaning
break	+	-able	=	breakable	able to be broken
danger	+	-ous	=	dangerous	full of danger

Add one of the suffixes above to the underlined noun or verb in the first of each pair of sentences. Then write the adjective you've made on the line to complete the second sentence. (*In number 15, drop the final *e* before you add the suffix.)

9. The library does not allow eating or drinking in the building.

Snacks are ______________________ only outside the library.

10. The skull and cross-bones is printed on all bottles of poison.

Children should not play with ______________________ liquids.

11. I want to wash my new sweater.

I am not sure if it is ______________________.

12. It took a lot of courage to save the children in the burning house.

The firefighters were very ______________________.

13. Carlos cannot afford to buy a new car.

A used car is much more ______________________.

14. The new business soon began to prosper.

It is now one of the most ______________________ businesses in town.

*** 15.** Hank Aaron's fame spread quickly after he broke Babe Ruth's home run record.

Aaron is one of the most ______________________ baseball players in history.

16. I really enjoy watching a baseball game.

It's one of the most ______________________ things I do all summer.

CHAPTER

Jesse Owens starts a race at the 1936 Olympics.

Jesse Owens: The Fastest Man

Reading Skill: Noticing the Sequence of Events

Expand Your Vocabulary: World War II

Get Ready to Read

1. How do you feel when someone says he or she can do something better than you? What do you say or do?

____

____

____

2. Look at the picture above and read the title of this chapter. Then read the first paragraph on the next page. What do you think you will learn when you read the essay?

____

____

____

Jesse Owens: The Fastest Man

In 1913, Jesse Owens, an African American, was born in a small Alabama town. His family was poor. But 23 years later, people all over the world knew his name. His actions showed everyone that the ideas of a powerful and dangerous leader were wrong.

When he was eight, Owens moved with his family to Cleveland, Ohio. There he became the star of his high school track team. As a senior, he set the high school record for the 100-yard dash.

Many colleges and universities tried to **recruit** Owens for their track teams. He decided to go to Ohio State University. At one college track competition, he did something amazing. First, he tied the world record for the 100-yard dash. Fifteen minutes later, he set a record in the long jump. During the next 40 minutes, he set world records in the 220-yard dash and the 220-yard low hurdles.

On the other side of the world, the leader of Germany, Adolf Hitler, was building a powerful army. His Nazi Party believed that white Germans were **superior** to all other people, especially Africans and Jews. Hitler believed that Germany should therefore rule the world. He spread this racist **propaganda** with government newspapers, huge rallies, and a violent police force. Hitler planned to use the 1936 Olympics in Berlin, the capital of Germany, to prove his beliefs. He expected German athletes to defeat athletes from other "**inferior**" races.

The United States sent 18 African-American athletes to the Olympics. Owens was one of them. He watched as Hitler entered the stadium with a large group of soldiers. The crowd of 100,000 people cheered and gave the Nazi salute.

Adolf Hitler gives the Nazi salute in the Olympic stadium.

Owens won the gold medal in his first event, the 100 meters, with a time of 10.3 seconds. After Owens won his second medal, Luz Long, a German athlete, put his arms around Owens to **congratulate** him on his win. The whole crowd was clapping for the young African American. Hitler was very angry. He left the stadium and refused to give out the medals. Owens won four gold medals and set three world records. He was the first American to win four gold medals in track and field in a single Olympics. In all, African Americans won 14 medals.

In 1976, Owens received another medal. President Gerald Ford gave Owens the Medal of Freedom. Owens died in 1980, but he will not be forgotten. The Jesse Owens Foundation gives money and **support** to young people trying to achieve their goals.

Jesse Owens jumps over a hurdle on this U.S. postage stamp.

Check Your Understanding

1. In what event did Jesse Owens set a new high school record?

____

2. How did the crowd at the Olympics react when Owens won more and more medals?

____

____

3. Why did Hitler become angry and leave the stadium?

____

____

Build Your Vocabulary

What is the meaning of each word in red? Fill in the correct bubble.

1. Many colleges and universities tried to **recruit** Owens for their track teams. He decided to go to Ohio State University.

   Ⓐ send someone away
   Ⓑ get someone to join a group
   Ⓒ scare someone
   Ⓓ pay someone to do something

2. His Nazi Party believed that white Germans were **superior** to all other people, especially Africans and Jews. Hitler believed that Germany should therefore rule the world.

   Ⓐ worse
   Ⓑ not good at all
   Ⓒ equally good
   Ⓓ better

3. He spread this racist **propaganda** with government newspapers, huge rallies, and a violent police force.

   Ⓐ interesting stories about people from around the world
   Ⓑ national news reports
   Ⓒ information that is supposed to make people believe something
   Ⓓ music and songs

4. He expected German athletes to defeat athletes from other "**inferior**" races.

   Ⓐ worse
   Ⓑ not good at all
   Ⓒ equally good
   Ⓓ better

5. After Owens won his second medal, Luz Long, a German athlete, put his arms around Owens to **congratulate** him on his win.

   Ⓐ ask someone for a favor
   Ⓑ make fun of someone
   Ⓒ protect someone from harm or injury
   Ⓓ tell someone you are happy about his or her achievement

6. The Jesse Owens Foundation gives money and **support** to young people trying to achieve their goals.

   Ⓐ medals
   Ⓑ help
   Ⓒ gifts
   Ⓓ explanations

Noticing the Sequence of Events

As you read, notice the *sequence of events,* or order in which things happen. Sometimes the writer will tell the date or time of an event. Words such as *then, next, later,* and *afterward* can also help you follow the sequence of events. For example:

> *In 1913,* Jesse Owens, an African American, was born in a small Alabama town . . . *23 years later,* people all over the world knew his name.

A sequence map like the one below lists events in the order in which they happened. Write these six events in the correct order in the sequence map. One has been done for you.

Hilter became angry and left the Olympic stadium.

Jesse Owens moved to Cleveland.

President Gerald Ford gave Jesse Owens the Medal of Freedom.

~~Jesse Owens set the high school record for the 100-yard dash.~~

Luz Long congratulated Jesse Owens for winning his second gold medal.

Jesse Owens went to Ohio State University.

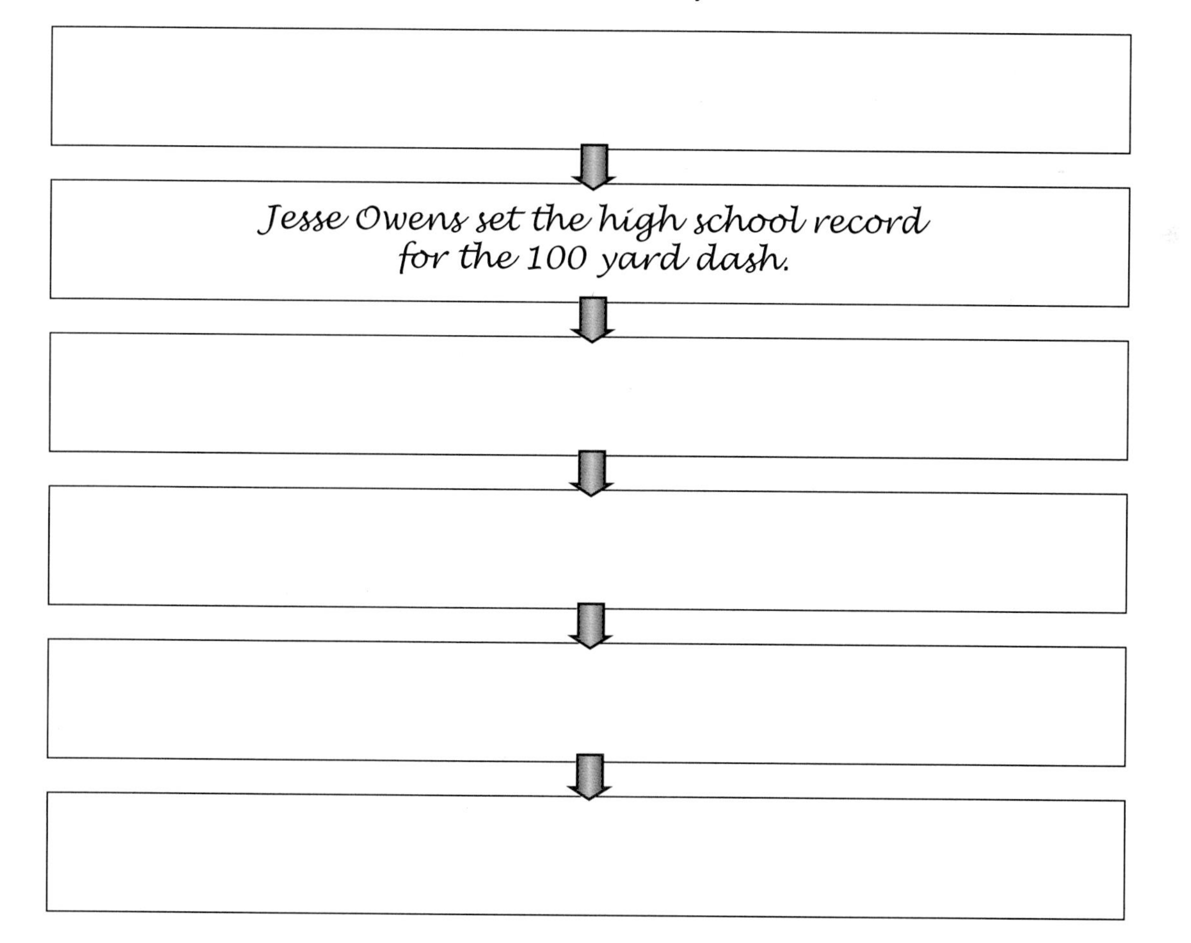

Expand Your Vocabulary

World War II

Read the definitions below of four words that relate to the Nazis in World War II.

fascism /ˈfæʃɪzəm/ *noun* a type of government that completely controls people's lives, does not allow disagreement, and says that its people are better than all other people

German fascism caused it to attack neighboring countries.

genocide /ˈdʒɛnəˌsaɪd/ *noun* the planned killing of an entire race or culture

Hitler ordered the genocide of Jews and Gypsies in areas he controlled.

ghetto /ˈgɛtoʊ/ *noun* a part of a city in which a specific group of people is forced to live

The Nazis forced Jews to live in crowded ghettos.

stereotype /ˈstɛriəˌtaɪp/ *noun* a belief that people have particular qualities because they are members of a particular race, sex, or culture

Jesse Owens proved that Hilter's stereotype of Africans was wrong.

True or False? Use the definitions. Fill in the correct bubble.

	True	False
1. Ghettos are places where people want to live.	Ⓣ	Ⓕ
2. Stereotypes can lead to unfair treatment of different groups.	Ⓣ	Ⓕ
3. Under fascism, all people are considered equal.	Ⓣ	Ⓕ
4. Genocide is the result of hatred between groups of people.	Ⓣ	Ⓕ

Put It in Writing

Write a paragraph about a false stereotype that people have of a particular group of people. It can be one that is present today or one that people had in the past. Tell why it is not true.

CHAPTER

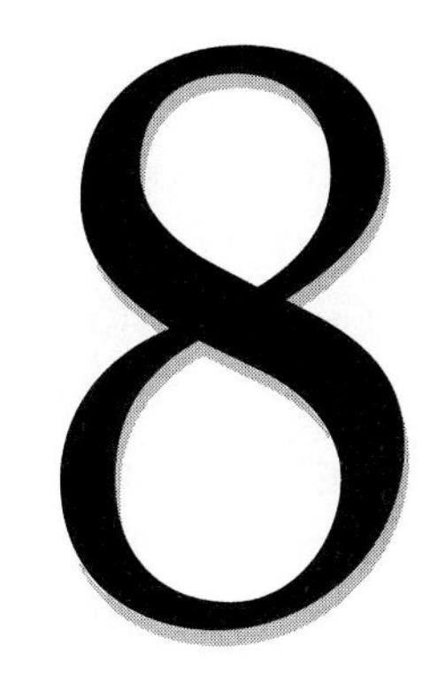

The U.S. battleship Arizona, *is sunk during the Japanese attack on Pearl Harbor.*

Pearl Harbor, December 7, 1941

Reading Skill:
Noticing Details

Expand Your Vocabulary:
Diplomacy

Get Ready to Read

1. List three things you know about the U.S. war with Japan in World War II. Form groups of three or four and share your lists.

____

____

____

2. Look at the picture above and read the title of this chapter. What do you think happened on December 7, 1941?

____

____

____

Pearl Harbor, December 7, 1941

1 Two large oceans separate the United States from Europe and Asia. For years, therefore, many people in the United States felt that trouble in other parts of the world, even war, was not their problem. But in 1940, the problems in Europe were getting worse and becoming a **crisis**. In 1939, Germany attacked 5 and took control of Poland. The next spring, German armies took over Denmark, Norway, the Netherlands, and Belgium. In June, France **surrendered**, and Germany started to bomb England.

On the other side of the world, Japan defeated China and was 10 **threatening** other nearby countries. Nearly everyone in the United States disagreed with the actions of Germany and Japan. Even so, many Americans did not 15 want the United States to fight in the war. President Franklin Roosevelt promised not to send U.S. troops into these **foreign** wars. But that soon changed.

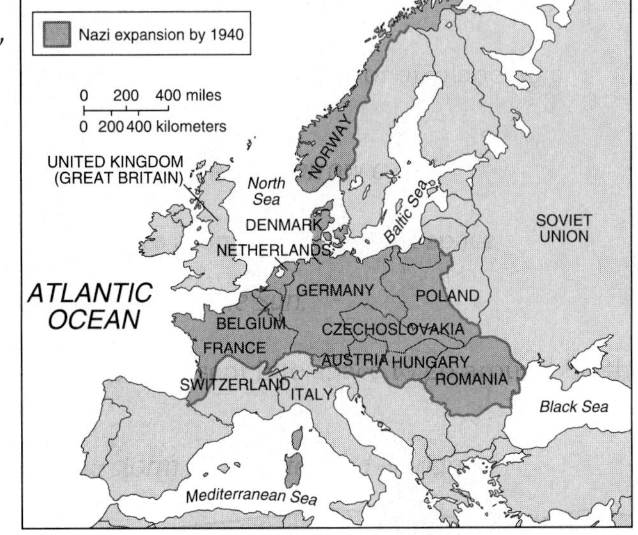

In 1940, the German Nazis controlled much of Europe.

20 To make it harder for the Japanese to make war, the United States refused to sell them oil and metals. The Japanese asked to meet with U.S. officials to discuss their disagreements. However, the Japanese were not interested in a peaceful solution. 25 Instead, they planned a surprise attack on Pearl Harbor, a large U.S. military base in the Hawaiian Islands.

Officials in the War Department 30 **suspected** an attack and sent a warning to the commander at Pearl Harbor. It arrived too late. At 7:53 A.M. on December 7, 1941, hundreds of Japanese planes began dropping 35 bombs on the ships in Pearl Harbor. They also attacked planes on a nearby airfield. The United States was caught by surprise.

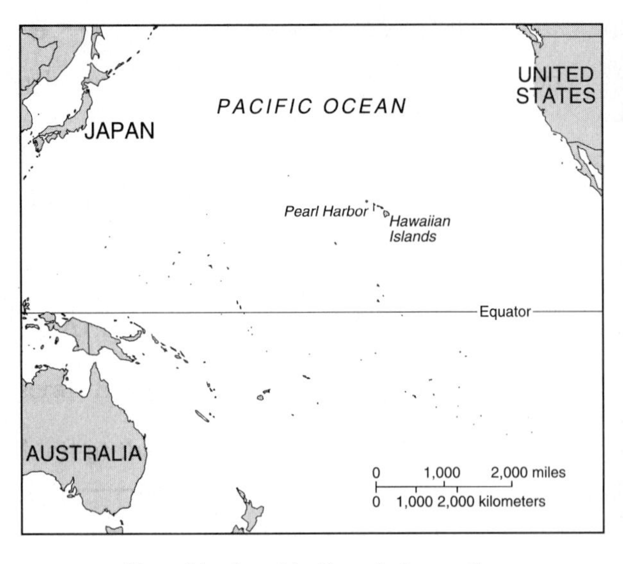

Hawaii is almost halfway between the United States and Japan.

For three hours, Pearl Harbor shook with explosions. Thick, black smoke and big flames rose from the ships. Planes were destroyed before they could get off the ground. A bomb hit the battleship *Arizona* and caused a huge explosion. The ship sank in nine minutes, trapping over 1,100 sailors inside. When the attack was over, 2,395 people were dead and 21 ships and 323 planes were damaged or destroyed.

The Arizona Memorial in Pearl Harbor, Hawaii

That night, President Roosevelt told the nation to expect a long and difficult war. He also warned that the United States could never again isolate itself from the rest of the world. It was a long and terrible war, but nearly four years later, on September 2, 1945, Japan surrendered.

In 1962, a special building was built over the **wreckage** of the *Arizona*. Visitors can see the rusted ship on the bottom of the harbor. The bodies of its sailors are still inside. Drops of oil from the *Arizona* continue to rise to the surface today. Some people think of them as the ship's tears.

Check Your Understanding

1. Why did many people in the United States feel that trouble in other parts of the world was not their problem?

___

___

___

2. Why did Japan want American oil and metals?

___

___

___

3. How did the Japanese trick the United States into thinking that they wanted peace?

___

___

___

Build Your Vocabulary

What is the meaning of each word in red? Fill in the correct bubble.

1. But in 1940, the problems in Europe were getting worse and becoming a **crisis**.

Ⓐ difficult and dangerous situation
Ⓑ peaceful and calm situation
Ⓒ famous story
Ⓓ agreement between two nations

2. The next spring, German armies took over Denmark, Norway, the Netherlands, and Belgium. In June, France **surrendered**, and Germany started to bomb England.

Ⓐ attacked
Ⓑ asked for help
Ⓒ gave up
Ⓓ won

3. On the other side of the world, Japan defeated China and was **threatening** other nearby countries.

Ⓐ trading with them
Ⓑ becoming friendly with them
Ⓒ joining them
Ⓓ saying that it was going to do something bad to them

4. Nearly everyone in the United States disagreed with the actions of Germany and Japan. Even so, many Americans did not want the United States to fight in the war. President Franklin Roosevelt promised not to send U.S. troops into these **foreign** wars.

Ⓐ in or from another country
Ⓑ unnecessary
Ⓒ unknown
Ⓓ illegal

5. Officials in the War Department **suspected** an attack and sent a warning to the commander at Pearl Harbor.

Ⓐ decided not to prepare for something
Ⓑ believed something unusual might be true but were not sure about it
Ⓒ decided to allow something
Ⓓ forgot about something

6. In 1962, a special building was built over the **wreckage** of the *Arizona*. Visitors can see the rusted ship on the bottom of the harbor.

Ⓐ statue for sailors who died in battle
Ⓑ type of photograph
Ⓒ place on a ship for keeping weapons
Ⓓ parts left after something is destroyed

Noticing Details

When you read, pay attention to *details*, the small pieces of information in a paragraph. The details often help you understand the big ideas better.

Work with a partner.

Student A: Read the first paragraph in the reading aloud.

Student B: Listen for the details and write the answers to questions 1 through 3.

Questions	Answers
1. What separates the United States from Europe and Asia?	
2. What were three countries that Germany took over by the end of 1940?	**a.** **b.** **c.**
3. Which country did Germany begin bombing in June 1940?	

Change jobs.

Student B: Read the fifth and sixth paragraph aloud.

Student A: Listen for the details and write the answers to questions 4 and 5.

Questions	Answers
4. What did the Japanese destroy at Pearl Harbor?	
5. What two things did President Franklin Roosevelt tell the nation after the attack?	**a.** **b.**

Expand Your Vocabulary

Diplomacy

Read the definitions below of four words that are related to diplomacy, or the way countries deal with each other.

ally /ˈæˌlaɪ/ *noun* a country that joins another country for a purpose, such as fighting a war

Russia was an ally of the United States in World War II.

ambassador /æmˈbæsədər/ *noun* an official who represents a government in another country

Mexico's ambassador to the United States met with the president.

liberate /ˈlɪbəˌreɪt/ *verb* to set someone free from prison or a government's control

The troops were able to liberate France from German control.

neutral /ˈnutrəl/ *adjective* not choosing sides in a war between other countries

The small country hoped to stay out of the war by being neutral.

Fill in each blank with the correct word from above.

1. After Japan attacked Pearl Harbor, the United States could not stay ____________________ in World War II.
2. The ____________________ delivered a message from his government.
3. Without a(n) ____________________, the weak country could not possibly win the war.
4. The prisoners were waiting for their army to ____________________ them.

Put It in Writing

Write a short newspaper story reporting the attack on Pearl Harbor. Be sure your story answers the questions Who? What? Where? When? and How? Include a short headline. Try to use one or more of the words above.

Vocabulary Tests

One type of test asks you to choose words that correctly complete sentences. The words often have something to do with time or the connection between two actions or ideas. Read the entire sentence and try out each word in the blank before choosing your answer.

Practice this strategy on these sample questions.

Directions: Choose the word that BEST completes each sentence. Fill in the circle below the answer you think is correct.

Sample Question

S1. Carlos wanted to go to the soccer game, ________________ he had too much homework to do.

perhaps	rather	if	but
Ⓐ	Ⓑ	Ⓒ	Ⓓ

Directions: Read these sentences. Then fill in the blanks with the correct words for numbers S2 through S4.

Sample Questions

Last night Josh and I **(S2)** ________________ to the movies. My mom gave me some **(S3)** ________________ for popcorn. **(S4)** ________________ the movie was over, she took us out for pizza.

S2.	**S3.**	**S4.**
Ⓐ go	Ⓐ theaters	Ⓐ After
Ⓑ went	Ⓑ friends	Ⓑ Although
Ⓒ saw	Ⓒ time	Ⓒ Next
Ⓓ looked	Ⓓ money	Ⓓ On

Did you always remember what the directions asked you to do? The correct answers are on page 122.

PRACTICE TEST

Choose the word that BEST completes each sentence. Fill in the circle below the answer you think is correct.

1. The school picnic will be in Lincoln Park. The picnic will be moved to the cafeteria ______________ it rains.

unless	if	because	maybe
Ⓐ	Ⓑ	Ⓒ	Ⓓ

2. Now that I ______________ learned to use the Internet, I can send messages to my friends.

may	since	have	having
Ⓐ	Ⓑ	Ⓒ	Ⓓ

3. Our class earned $250 by washing cars on Saturday. We'll use the money to buy new uniforms ______________ our basketball team.

at	about	without	for
Ⓐ	Ⓑ	Ⓒ	Ⓓ

Read these sentences. Then fill in the blanks with the correct words for numbers 4 through 9.

Yesterday my teacher **(4)**______________ me to get a book from the library. She wants me to read **(5)**______________ and to write a report on the book by **(6)**______________ week.

4. Ⓐ asked Ⓑ asks Ⓒ asking Ⓓ ask

5. Ⓐ them Ⓑ those Ⓒ her Ⓓ it

6. Ⓐ next Ⓑ last Ⓒ before Ⓓ until

No one has **(7)**______________ Jim for several days. It has been almost a week **(8)**______________ I talked to him. Maybe **(9)**______________ sick.

7. Ⓐ saw Ⓑ seen Ⓒ sees Ⓓ scene

8. Ⓐ without Ⓑ whenever Ⓒ since Ⓓ because

9. Ⓐ he's Ⓑ hes Ⓒ his Ⓓ he

Correct answers are on page 122.

STOP

CHAPTER

Cesar Chavez leads a group of striking farm workers in the 1960s.

Cesar Chavez and the United Farm Workers

Reading Skill:
Finding Main Ideas and Supporting Details

Expand Your Vocabulary:
Business and Labor

Get Ready to Read

1. What are some hard jobs people have today? What makes them difficult?

____

____

____

2. Look at the picture above and read the title of this chapter. What changes do you think these farm workers wanted?

____

____

____

Cesar Chavez and the United Farm Workers

1 Picking fruit and vegetables is very hard work. Workers bend over rows of lettuce or stand on ladders to reach fruit all day long. The weather is hot. Poisons for killing insects sometimes make the workers sick. Then when all the fruit or vegetables are picked, the job is over. Workers must move to another farm to find 5 more work. Workers move often, and their children change schools many times.

Farm workers in a lettuce field

During the Great Depression, farm work was the only job that many people could find. They therefore had to accept low pay and very bad living conditions. And 30 years later, conditions were still not better. In 1962, one Mexican American worker named Cesar Chavez decided to try to change that.

10 Chavez took several nonviolent actions to bring about change. First he started an organization of workers called a **union**. He traveled to fields throughout California to ask workers to join his organization. By 1965, his union had 1,700 members, but farm owners refused to talk to them. That year Chavez's union joined another union in a **strike** against grape growers and refused to pick 15 grapes. The new organization was called the United Farm Workers (UFW). The grape growers, however, did not want to talk to the UFW. The union needed a way to get the growers to listen to their demands. Chavez decided to ask Americans not to buy grapes until the growers met with the UFW.

UFW members marched 340 miles to the California capital to **publicize** 20 their problem. Hundreds more workers visited towns and cities across the

United States to ask people not to buy grapes. People supported the **boycott**, and the sales of grapes went down.

Little by little, grape growers began signing agreements with the UFW. But that did not end the workers' problems. When the agreements **expired**, many growers tried legal tricks to avoid signing new agreements. The UFW had to begin another series of boycotts. By 1975, one expert estimated that 17 million shoppers were refusing to buy grapes. Then in 1975, Chavez got the California government to pass a law that gave farm workers the right to form unions and **negotiate** with growers.

When Cesar Chavez died in 1993, he was still working to make better lives for farm workers. His jacket now hangs in the National Museum of American History in Washington, D.C. A "No Grapes" button is pinned to the front of it.

The "No Grapes" symbol used by the United Farm Workers

Check Your Understanding

1. List two things that make picking fruit and vegetables hard work.

____

____

____

2. Why didn't the grape growers want to talk to Cesar Chavez and his union?

____

____

____

3. How did the United Farm Workers get the grape growers to sign agreements with them?

____

____

____

Build Your Vocabulary

What is the meaning of each word in red? Fill in the correct bubble.

1. Chavez took several nonviolent actions to bring about change. First he started an organization of workers called a **union**.

- (A) group that manages grape growers
- (B) agreement signed by grape growers and workers
- (C) school for the children of farm workers
- (D) group that speaks for workers

2. That year Chavez's union joined another union in a **strike** against grape growers and refused to pick grapes.

- (A) period of time when workers stop working to protest
- (B) agreement
- (C) meeting to discuss working conditions
- (D) law passed by a state

3. UFW members marched 340 miles to the California capital to **publicize** their problem. Hundreds more workers visited towns and cities across the United States to ask people not to buy grapes.

- (A) send something away
- (B) give out information about something to a lot of people
- (C) keep something hidden from others
- (D) blame the government for something

4. Hundreds more workers visited towns and cities across the United States to ask people not to buy grapes. People supported the **boycott**, and the sales of grapes went down.

- (A) money paid to farm owners for their fruit and vegetables
- (B) young men who work in the fields
- (C) action of refusing to buy or use something
- (D) vote by members of a group

5. When the agreements **expired**, many growers tried legal tricks to avoid signing new agreements.

- (A) needed help
- (B) improved
- (C) stopped being good or legal
- (D) became longer

6. Then in 1975, Chavez got the California legislature to pass a law that gave farm workers the right to form unions and **negotiate** with growers.

- (A) refuse to meet
- (B) discuss disagreements
- (C) buy and sell
- (D) go to school

Finding Main Ideas and Supporting Details

The *main idea* of a paragraph is the most important idea. The *supporting details* give information that helps you understand the main ideas.

1. The main idea of this paragraph from the reading selection has been underlined. Work with a partner and list four supporting details.

> Picking fruit and vegetables is very hard work. Workers bend over rows of lettuce or stand on ladders to reach fruit all day long. The weather is hot. Poisons for killing insects sometimes make the workers sick. Then when all the fruit or vegetables are picked, the job is over. Workers must move to another farm to find more work. Workers move often and their children change schools many times.

Main Idea: *Picking fruit and vegetables is very hard work.*

Supporting Detail: ____________________

Supporting Detail: ____________________

Supporting Detail: ____________________

Supporting Detail: ____________________

2. Read paragraph 3 on page 58 again. Write the sentence that states the main idea of the paragraph. Then write three supporting details for the main idea.

Main Idea: ____________________

____

Supporting Detail: ____________________

Supporting Detail: ____________________

Supporting Detail: ____________________

Expand Your Vocabulary

Business and Labor

Read the definitions below of four words that are related to business and labor.

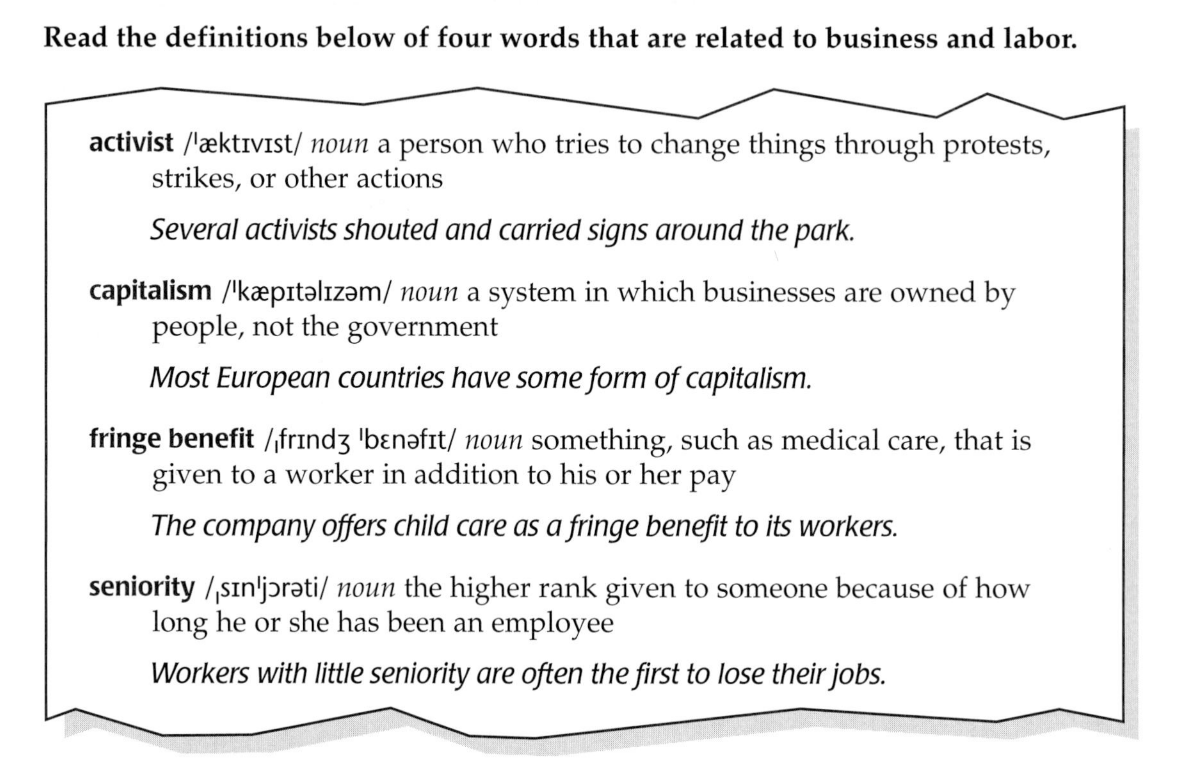

activist /ˈæktɪvɪst/ *noun* a person who tries to change things through protests, strikes, or other actions

Several activists shouted and carried signs around the park.

capitalism /ˈkæpɪtəlɪzəm/ *noun* a system in which businesses are owned by people, not the government

Most European countries have some form of capitalism.

fringe benefit /ˌfrɪndʒ ˈbɛnəfɪt/ *noun* something, such as medical care, that is given to a worker in addition to his or her pay

The company offers child care as a fringe benefit to its workers.

seniority /ˌsɪnˈjɔrəti/ *noun* the higher rank given to someone because of how long he or she has been an employee

Workers with little seniority are often the first to lose their jobs.

Write the correct word from above next to each clue.

_______________________ **1.** Because of this system, you can start your own business if you want to.

_______________________ **2.** If you have worked for a company for 20 years, you have more of this than someone who has worked there for just a year.

_______________________ **3.** You might become this if you are not happy with a situation in society and want to change it.

_______________________ **4.** A vacation from work with pay is an example of this.

Put It in Writing

Write an advertisement for the Work Wanted part of a newspaper. Tell what kind of job you would like. Also tell what you want from a company that hires you. Try to use one or more of the words above.

President John F. Kennedy in front of U.S. missiles during the time of the Cuban Missile Crisis in 1962

CHAPTER

The Cuban Missile Crisis

Reading Skill: Noticing the Sequence of Events

Expand Your Vocabulary: War and Peace

Get Ready to Read

1. Where is Cuba located? List three things you know about Cuba. Meet in groups of three or four and share what you know about Cuba.

____

____

____

2. Read the title of this chapter. Why do you think missiles in Cuba caused a crisis?

____

____

____

The Cuban Missile Crisis

After World War II, the United States and the Soviet Union were the two most powerful countries in the world. The Soviet Union tried to use its power to spread its form of government: communism. The United States strongly **opposed** new communist governments. As a result, the two countries often threatened each other with angry words and **hostile** actions. Both countries had powerful nuclear weapons. An accident or even a small **conflict** could possibly start a huge nuclear war. In October 1962 that nearly happened.

At 8:45 A.M., on October 16, President John F. Kennedy learned that the Soviet Union was putting missiles in Cuba. Cuba is a communist country just 90 miles from Florida. Those missiles could hit nearly every city in the United States. If the missiles carried nuclear weapons, 85 million Americans could be killed.

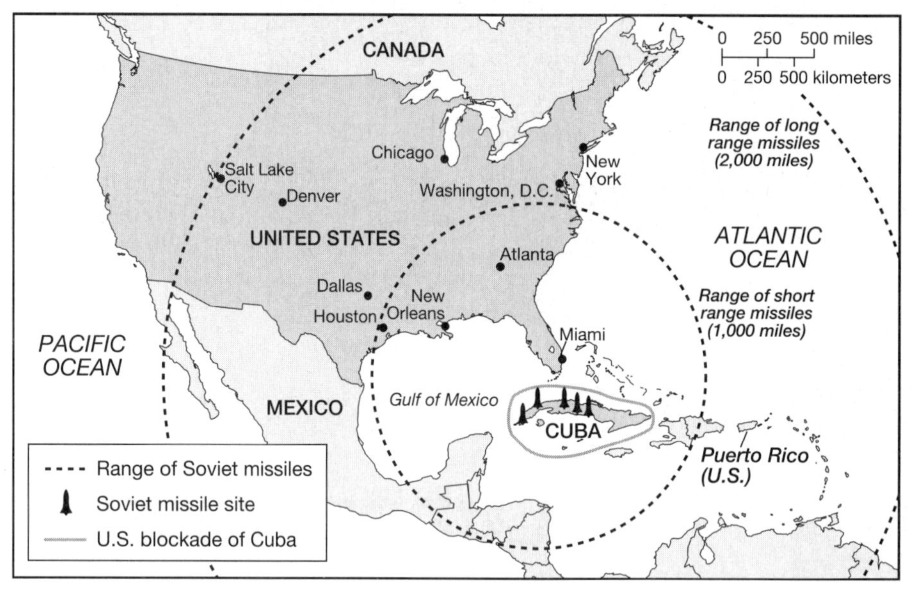

The Cuban missiles could reach much of the United States.

For hours President Kennedy and his **advisers** talked about what to do. The United States could just wait and do nothing, but no one at the meeting thought that that was a good idea. Some advisers told the president to send planes to destroy the missiles. Most felt that was too dangerous. It could easily lead to nuclear war. Both countries would be completely destroyed. No one wanted that, but everyone agreed that the United States had to do something.

President Kennedy decided on a **compromise** between doing nothing and attacking the missiles. In a speech on television, he told the nation that the U.S. navy was going to stop all ships carrying missiles to Cuba. If the ships refused to stop, the navy was going to sink them.

As 24 Soviet ships sailed toward Cuba, the world waited in fear. U.S. warships rushed to stop the Soviet ships. U.S. planes with nuclear bombs were ready to attack. Some Americans hid in bomb shelters under the ground.

Two days after the president's speech all the Soviet ships stopped. Some turned back, but there were still missiles in Cuba. Then the Soviet Union sent a message to President Kennedy. It promised to remove the missiles if the United States promised never to attack Cuba. The United States agreed. The next day the Soviet military began to remove the missiles. Little by little, the world began to relax.

After the crisis, the United States and the Soviet Union signed the first **treaty** to control tests of nuclear weapons. This did not end the chance of a nuclear war, but it helped make the world a little safer.

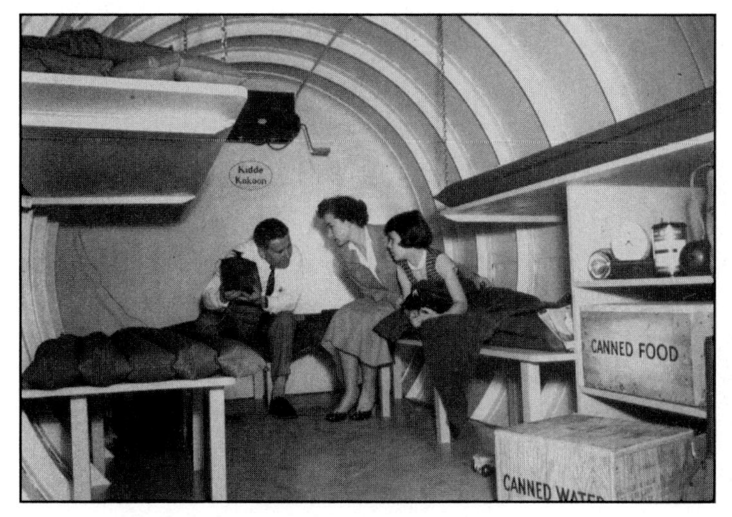

An American family in a bomb shelter in the 1960s

Check Your Understanding

1. What kind of government did the Soviet Union have in 1962?

____

____

2. What did President John F. Kennedy decide to do about the missiles in Cuba?

____

____

3. Why did some people in the United States hide in bomb shelters during the Cuban Missile Crisis?

____

____

____

Build Your Vocabulary

What is the meaning of each word in red? Fill in the correct bubble.

1. The Soviet Union tried to use its power to spread its form of government: communism. The United States strongly **opposed** new communist governments. As a result, the two countries often threatened each other with angry words and hostile actions.

- (A) welcomed
- (B) studied
- (C) fought against
- (D) gave help to

2. As a result, the two countries often threatened each other with angry words and **hostile** actions.

- (A) tricky
- (B) unusual
- (C) very unfriendly
- (D) hidden

3. Both countries had powerful nuclear weapons. An accident or even a small **conflict** could possibly start a huge nuclear war.

- (A) agreement
- (B) disagreement or fight
- (C) weapon
- (D) government

4. For hours President Kennedy and his **advisers** talked about what to do.

- (A) people who help someone make a decision
- (B) companies that make nuclear weapons
- (C) people who do not agree with a decision
- (D) people who are elected to government jobs

5. President Kennedy decided on a **compromise** between doing nothing and attacking the missiles.

- (A) decision that is completely different from other ones
- (B) long discussion
- (C) period of time when nothing is done
- (D) decision in which everyone gives up part of what he or she wants

6. After the crisis, the United States and the Soviet Union signed the first **treaty** to control tests of nuclear weapons.

- (A) agreement between two or more countries
- (B) check for a lot of money
- (C) long letter
- (D) book

Noticing the Sequence of Events

As you read, notice the *sequence of events,* or order in which things happen. Sometimes the writer will tell the date or time of an event. Dates and words such as *then* and *next* help you to follow the order in which things happen.

Read the list of events below. Then write the events in the order in which they happened on the lines. One has been done for you.

~~The United States agreed not to attack Cuba if the Soviet Union removed the missiles.~~

The United States and the Soviet Union signed a treaty to control tests of nuclear weapons.

President Kennedy talked with his advisers.

President Kennedy decided to stop all ships carrying missiles to Cuba.

President Kennedy learned that the Soviet Union was putting missiles in Cuba.

The 24 Soviet ships sailing to Cuba stopped or turned back.

1. ______________________________

2. ______________________________

3. ______________________________

4. ______________________________

5. The United States agreed not to attack Cuba if the Soviet Union removed the missiles.

6. ______________________________

Expand Your Vocabulary

War and Peace

Read the definitions below of four words that relate to war and peace.

alliance /əˈlaɪəns/ *noun* an agreement between two or more countries to help each other

Spain and Portugal formed an alliance in order to help each other in time of war.

blockade /blɑˈkeɪd/ *noun* an action of using military force to stop supplies from entering or leaving a place

During the Civil War, Union ships placed a blockade on Southern harbors.

diplomacy /dɪˈploʊməsi/ *noun* the skill to arrange agreements between nations

Thanks to the ambassador's diplomacy, the two countries settled their disagreements.

superpower /ˈsupərˌpaʊər/ *noun* a powerful nation, especially one that has nuclear weapons

The nation hoped to become a superpower in less than 10 years.

True or False? Use the definitions. Fill in the correct bubble.

	True	False
1. A blockade is an unfriendly action.	(T)	(F)
2. A superpower does not have an army or navy.	(T)	(F)
3. Before a nation goes to war, it might try diplomacy.	(T)	(F)
4. Weaker countries might form an alliance to fight a superpower.	(T)	(F)

Put It in Writing

Write a short report about the Cuban Missile Crisis or another crisis that a newsman or newswoman might read on the radio. Try to use one or more of the words above.

Word Parts and Meanings

You see certain word parts in many words. Knowing the meaning of these word parts will help you figure out the meanings of many words.

The trucks **transport** food across the country.

Kip took his **portable** radio to the beach.

When you see *port* in a word, the word may have something to do with carrying something.

Underline the shared word part you find in the red words in each set of three sentences. Then write what you think the word part means or is related to. The first one has been started for you.

1. You should add some color to the poster to make it more **visually** interesting.
   The marks are almost **invisible**—you have to look very closely to see them.
   If you are having problems with your **vision**, you should go to an eye doctor.
   vis = ______________________

2. The doctor wrote a **prescription** for me so I could get the medicine I need.
   The writer sent the **manuscript** of her new book to a publisher.
   I read a **transcript** of the senator's speech in the newspaper.
   ____

3. I fell from my bike when my foot slipped off the **pedal**.
   The cars stopped to let the **pedestrians** cross the street.
   The **centipede** moved its many legs quickly as it climbed up the wall.
   ____

4. The **symphony** will perform a concert in the park on Saturday.
   Alexander Graham Bell invented the **telephone** in 1876.
   The speaker clipped a small **microphone** to his collar.
   ____

5. Over 1,000 **spectators** watched the baseball game.
   Let's ask the mechanic to **inspect** the car's brakes.
   If you look at the statue from a different **perspective**, you will notice new things.
   ____

Word Part	Meaning	Word Part	Meaning	Word Part	Meaning
auto	self	graph	write	scope	look at
bio	life	logy	study	tele	far
geo	earth	micro	small	therm	heat

Use the list of word parts and meanings above to match the words below with their meanings.

_______________ **1.** autobiography

_______________ **2.** thermometer

_______________ **3.** biography

_______________ **4.** geology

_______________ **5.** telescope

_______________ **6.** microbiology

_______________ **7.** microscope

_______________ **8.** geothermal

_______________ **9.** telegraph

_______________ **10.** autograph

a. a machine for sending a written message a long distance

b. related to heat that comes from the Earth

c. a famous person's name written by that person

d. an instrument for looking at things that are very far away

e. the study of small living things

f. the study of the Earth

g. the story of someone's life that is written by another person

h. an instrument that measures how hot something is

i. the story of someone's life that is written by that person

j. an instrument for looking at very small things

Martin Luther King, Jr. prepares to give a speech at the Lincoln Memorial in Washington, D.C., on August 28, 1963.

CHAPTER

Martin Luther King, Jr.'s Dream

Reading Skill:
Making Inferences

Expand Your Vocabulary:
The Civil Rights Movement

Get Ready to Read

1. Do you think some laws treat people unfairly? List any laws you think are unfair. What can people in the United States do to change unfair laws like these? Form groups of three or four and share your ideas.

____

____

____

2. Read the title of this chapter and the first paragraph on the next page. What do you think Martin Luther King, Jr.'s dream was?

____

____

Martin Luther King, Jr.'s Dream

In the early 1950s, a girl named Linda Brown lived near an elementary school. But she had to take a long bus ride to go to another school. Linda Brown was African American. The school near her home was only for white children. At that time, laws in much of the United States, especially the South, prohibited African-American children from going to school with white children. Linda's father felt this was unfair. The Supreme Court agreed. It **ordered** states to let African Americans into white schools.

Some southern states found ways to avoid obeying the Court's order. Even so, the Court's decision **inspired** African Americans to demand fair treatment and equality in other things. In Montgomery, Alabama, Rosa Parks, an African American, refused to give her seat on a bus to a white man. She was arrested. African Americans decided to boycott the buses. They elected a young minister named Martin Luther King, Jr. as their leader. King promised to work for change peacefully. The boycott worked. The city agreed never again to tell African Americans where to sit on its buses.

King then led marches that called attention to **discrimination** against African Americans in other ways. He and his supporters were often beaten and sprayed with powerful hoses. Their homes were bombed, and some people

Martin Luther King, Jr. leads the march in Washington, D.C.

were murdered. Change came very slowly, if it happened at all. In 1963,
20 President John F. Kennedy decided that the country needed a strong **civil rights** law to make sure all Americans got equal rights and treatment. The president asked Congress to make discrimination in jobs, education, and the use of public places illegal. **Representatives** in Congress from southern states opposed the law.

25 Civil rights leaders decided to hold a march on Washington, D.C., to show support for a civil rights law. On August 28, 1963, more than 250,000 people of all races gathered at the Lincoln Memorial. King's speech that day is one of the most famous in American history. In it he described his dream for America:

> I have a dream that my four little children will one day
> 30 live in a nation where they will not be judged by the
> color of their skin but by the content of their character.

In other words, people's talents and qualities should matter, not their skin color. A year later, Congress passed a civil rights law.

35 Less than five years later in 1968, a man with a gun **assassinated** King. On King's grave are words from the end of his famous speech. In 1983, the third Monday in January was made a national holiday to honor King and his work to end discrimination.

Check Your Understanding

1. Why didn't Linda Brown go to the school near her home?

____

____

2. What law did Montgomery, Alabama, change because of the bus boycott?

____

____

3. What was the purpose of the march in Washington, D.C.?

____

____

Build Your Vocabulary

What is the meaning of each word in red? Fill in the correct bubble.

1. Linda's father felt this was unfair. The Supreme Court agreed. It **ordered** states to let African Americans into white schools.

- (A) stopped someone from doing something
- (B) scared someone into doing something
- (C) officially told someone to do something
- (D) helped someone do something

2. Some southern states found ways to avoid obeying the Court's order. Even so, the Court's decision **inspired** African Americans to demand fair treatment and equality in other things.

- (A) made someone weaker
- (B) asked someone
- (C) frightened someone
- (D) caused a strong feeling in someone

3. The city agreed never again to tell African Americans where to sit on its buses. King then led marches that called attention to **discrimination** against African Americans in other ways.

- (A) unfair treatment for a particular group of people
- (B) laws that tell people where to sit on buses
- (C) groups of people working to change a law
- (D) schools for African Americans

4. In 1963, President John F. Kennedy decided that the country needed a strong **civil rights** law to make sure all Americans got equal rights and treatment.

- (A) freedom to protest unfair laws
- (B) right to go to nearby schools
- (C) right to a job with good pay
- (D) freedoms that everyone in society should have

5. The president asked Congress to make discrimination in jobs, education, and the use of public places illegal. **Representatives** in Congress from southern states opposed the law.

- (A) people from the South
- (B) people who are elected to make decisions for other people
- (C) ordinary people
- (D) people who do not like other races

6. Less than five years later in 1968, a man with a gun **assassinated** King. On King's grave are words from the end of his famous speech.

- (A) suddenly replaced someone
- (B) killed someone important
- (C) gave an honor to someone
- (D) elected someone

Making Inferences

You can sometimes use facts that are stated directly to guess certain facts that are not stated. This is called *making inferences*. Making inferences helps you understand more of what you read.

Stated Fact: Some southern states found ways to avoid obeying the Court's order.

Inference: Some southern states did not like the Court's order.

Which inference can you make from each stated fact? Fill in the correct bubble.

1. In Montgomery, Alabama, Rosa Parks, an African American, refused to give her seat on a bus to a white man. She was arrested.

Ⓐ Montgomery, Alabama, has small buses.

Ⓑ There was a law that made African Americans give up their seats to white people.

2. African Americans decided to boycott the buses. They elected a young minister named Martin Luther King, Jr. as their leader. King promised to work for change peacefully.

Ⓐ African Americans hoped a boycott would bring change peacefully.

Ⓑ King was a great leader.

3. He and his supporters were frequently beaten and sprayed with powerful hoses. Their homes were bombed, and some people were murdered.

Ⓐ Some people hated King and his followers.

Ⓑ King had many followers in the South.

4. Change came very slowly, if it happened at all. In 1963, President John F. Kennedy decided that a strong civil rights law was needed.

Ⓐ Passing a civil rights law was going to be difficult.

Ⓑ Kennedy thought only a new law could change things.

5. Civil rights leaders decided to hold a march in Washington, D.C., to show support for a civil rights law. On August 28, 1963, more than 250,000 people of all races gathered at the Lincoln Memorial.

Ⓐ There was a lot of support for the civil rights law among all people.

Ⓑ The Lincoln Memorial is the best place to hold a march.

Expand Your Vocabulary

The Civil Rights Movement

Read the definitions below of four words that are related to the civil rights movement.

integrate /ˈɪntəˌgreɪt/ *verb* to include all races in the same schools, jobs, housing, and other places

In the late 1950s, the South began to slowly integrate its schools.

Jim Crow /ˌdʒɪm ˈkroʊ/ *noun* a system of rules or customs in the past of discriminating against African Americans

Under Jim Crow, African Americans had to pay a high tax before they were allowed to vote.

segregation /ˌsɛgrəˈgeɪʃən/ *noun* the practice of separating the races in schools, jobs, housing, and other places

In 1954, the Supreme Court ruled that segregation in the public schools was unfair to African Americans.

sit-in /ˈsɪtˌɪn/ *noun* a way of protesting something by sitting down as a group in a place and refusing to move

Civil rights workers held a sit-in at a restaurant that would not serve African Americans.

A sit-in

Write the correct word from above next to each clue.

______________________________ **1.** This is a peaceful way to call attention to something you think needs to be changed.

______________________________ **2.** Some southern governments used this system to limit the rights of African Americans.

______________________________ **3.** The Supreme Court ordered schools to do this in 1954.

______________________________ **4.** This kept students of different races from going to the same schools.

Put It in Writing

Write a poster or advertisement asking others to join you to protest an unfair law or practice. Try to use one or more of the words above.

Apollo 11 blasts off from Florida to the Moon on July 16, 1969.

CHAPTER

The Race to the Moon

Reading Skill:
Noticing Cause and Effect

Expand Your Vocabulary:
Space Travel

Get Ready to Read

1. Have you ever been the first person in your family or group of friends to do something exciting or difficult? If so, what was it? Why do people like to be the first to do things such as climb a tall mountain or go to the Moon?

___

___

___

2. What problems do you think scientists had to solve before they could send someone to the Moon?

___

___

___

The Race to the Moon

In 1961, President John F. Kennedy made an important speech. In it, he told the nation that he thought the United States should send a man to the Moon by 1970. Such an amazing and dangerous **mission** was going to require great scientific skill and huge amounts of money. Even then, no one was sure such a dangerous trip was going to **succeed**.

The reason for President Kennedy's speech was clear. One month earlier, the Soviet Union sent the first man into space. He went around Earth and returned safely. Until then, the United States believed it was the country with the most scientific knowledge in the world. The success of the Soviet spacecraft made people wonder if this belief was true. Americans wanted to prove that their scientists were superior. But they had to send a man to the Moon before the Soviet Union could get a man there.

Congress agreed to spend more money for space exploration. Work on a U.S. spacecraft began to go faster. A few months later, astronaut John Glenn went around Earth three times in a spacecraft named *Friendship 7*. Other U.S. astronauts completed several more successful trips. The U.S. space program was doing well. Then something terrible happened. In 1967, a fire trapped and killed three astronauts as they tested a new spacecraft. The space program was stopped for a year.

Meanwhile the Soviet Union was also **encountering** problems. A Soviet astronaut died when his parachute did not open during a landing. After these accidents, U.S. and Soviet scientists worked even harder. Finally, the United States was ready to try to send men to the Moon. Neil Armstrong and two other astronauts blasted off from Florida in *Apollo 11* on July 16, 1969. They took with them pieces of the airplane flown by the Wright Brothers in 1903. In Washington, D.C., President Richard Nixon prepared a speech in case the mission failed. He never had to use it. Four days later, on July 20, Armstrong walked on the Moon. After exploring and **performing** several experiments, the astronauts returned to Earth. The dangerous 238,000-mile (383,000-kilometer) trip to the Moon was a complete success. Unfortunately, the president who **encouraged** the nation to go to the Moon did not live to see it happen. President Kennedy was assassinated in 1963.

When Armstrong **departed** from the Moon, he left behind a U.S. flag. He took with him 46 pounds of Moon rock. You can see some of these rocks at the National Air and Space Museum in Washington, D.C.

Neil Armstrong walks on the Moon, July 20, 1969.

Check Your Understanding

1. What was *Friendship 7*?

____

____

2. Why did the United States stop its space program for a year?

____

____

3. President Richard Nixon had a speech ready in case the trip to the Moon failed. What does this show you about the trip?

____

____

____

Build Your Vocabulary

What is the meaning of each word in red? Fill in the correct bubble.

1. President John F. Kennedy told the nation that he thought the U.S. should send a man to the Moon by 1970. Such an amazing and dangerous **mission** would require great scientific skill and huge amounts of money.

   Ⓐ scientist
   Ⓑ speech that the president makes
   Ⓒ spacecraft
   Ⓓ important job someone gives you

2. Such an amazing and dangerous mission was going to require great scientific skill and huge amounts of money. Even then, no one was sure such a dangerous trip was going to **succeed**.

   Ⓐ do what people wanted it to do
   Ⓑ spend enough money
   Ⓒ make someone happy
   Ⓓ cause a problem

3. Meanwhile the Soviet Union was also **encountering** problems. A Soviet astronaut died when his parachute did not open during a landing.

   Ⓐ solving quickly
   Ⓑ starting to have
   Ⓒ giving away
   Ⓓ enjoying

4. After exploring and **performing** several experiments, the astronauts returned to Earth.

   Ⓐ choosing
   Ⓑ hiding
   Ⓒ doing
   Ⓓ throwing away

5. Unfortunately, the president who **encouraged** the nation to go to the Moon did not live to see it happen.

   Ⓐ begged someone to do something
   Ⓑ warned someone against something
   Ⓒ told someone that he or she should do something
   Ⓓ talked to someone about something

6. When Armstrong **departed** from the Moon, he left behind a U.S. flag.

   Ⓐ arrived
   Ⓑ went away
   Ⓒ flew
   Ⓓ escaped

Noticing Cause and Effect

A *cause* is the reason something happens. An *effect* is the thing that happens. An effect can sometimes be the cause of another effect.

Cause: The Soviet Union sent the first man into space.

Effect: People wondered if the United States had the most scientific knowledge.

Words such as *as a result, because, for that reason, so,* and *therefore* signal a cause and an effect.

Write the letter of the effect in column 2 next to its cause in column 1. The first one has been done for you.

Cause	Effect
d **1.** President John F. Kennedy asked the nation to send a man to the Moon and back.	**a.** So work on the U.S. spacecraft began to go faster.
____ **2.** Congress decided to spend money to explore space.	**b.** So he prepared a speech to announce a possible failure.
____ **3.** Fire killed three U.S. astronauts.	**c.** Therefore, scientists from the two countries had to work even harder.
____ **4.** Both the U.S. and Soviet space programs had problems.	**d.** As a result, Congress decided to spend money to explore space.
____ **5.** President Richard Nixon feared the mission might fail.	**e.** For that reason, work on the U.S. spacecraft stopped for a year.

Expand Your Vocabulary

Space Travel

Read the definitions below of four words that are related to space travel.

lunar /ˈlunər/ *adjective* related to the Moon

With the telescope, we could see the lunar mountains.

navigate /ˈnævɪˌgeɪt/ *verb* to guide an object, such as a ship or airplane, to a particular place

The captain had to navigate his ship through the narrow canal.

orbit /ˈɔrbɪt/ *noun* the path something takes around an object in space

Each planet follows a different orbit around the Sun.

satellite /ˈsætəˌlaɪt/ *noun* a piece of equipment sent into space to go around Earth and send back information

The satellite sent pictures of a large storm moving toward Florida.

Fill in each blank with the correct word from above to complete this newspaper story from 1969.

Neil Armstrong Walks on the Moon

Houston At 4:18 P.M. Eastern Standard Time today, Neil Armstrong stepped on the **(1)**________________ surface. Only 12 years ago the Soviet Union put the first **(2)**________________ in a(n) **(3)**________________ around the Earth. Since then, the United States has worked hard to be the first to go to the Moon. Today that race was won when Armstrong was able to **(4)**________________ his spacecraft *Eagle* to a safe landing between large rocks. He had just 30 seconds of fuel left at the time.

Put It in Writing

Write a paragraph to describe what the astronauts might have seen on the way to the Moon. Try to use one or more of the words above.

Reading Tests

Often the directions for a test question will include a key word, such as BEST, SAME, OPPOSITE, NOT, or MOST. The word will usually be in capital letters. Always pay close attention to this word. It tells you exactly what you must do to answer the question correctly.

Practice this strategy on the sample reading selection and questions below.

Directions: Read the selection below. Choose the BEST answer to the questions.

Apollo 11 was the first flight to put men on the Moon, but it was not the first flight to go to the Moon. That flight was *Apollo 8*. On December 21, 1968, three astronauts on *Apollo 8* took off from Cape Kennedy, Florida, and circled Earth one and a half times. Then they headed toward the Moon. On Christmas Day, they circled the Moon. The pictures the astronauts sent back made people look at Earth in a new way. For the first time people saw Earth hanging in space like a tiny blue ball. They saw themselves as tiny dots in a huge universe. They also saw the importance of protecting that blue water and rich land in a whole new way.

Sample Questions

S1. Which of these sentences BEST summarizes the paragraph?

- (A) On Christmas Day, astronauts circled the Moon.
- (B) People saw themselves as tiny dots in a huge universe.
- (C) *Apollo 8*'s flight was nearly as important as *Apollo 11*'s flight.
- (D) *Apollo 8* was a dangerous mission.

S2. Which of these is NOT mentioned in the paragraph?

- (A) the flight of *Apollo 11*
- (B) Christmas Day
- (C) Earth's water
- (D) *Apollo 8*'s return flight

Did you pay close attention to the words in large letters? The correct answers are on page 122.

PRACTICE TEST

Directions: Read the selection below. Choose the BEST answer to each question.

Scientists dream of sending someone to Mars, the planet closest to Earth. Going to Mars, however, will be very difficult. Mars is more then 200 times farther away than the Moon. The trip will take six months. All that time, the astronauts will be exposed to dangerous solar winds and harmful light waves. In 1989, scientists proposed building a giant spacecraft in orbit. This spacecraft could then travel to Mars. Astronauts would land and leave the spacecraft to explore the planet for long periods of time. They would then reenter the spacecraft and blast off for the six-month return trip. The cost for this trip is estimated to be $400 billion. This is much too expensive. A cheaper way has to be found. Scientists are still working on the problem.

1. What is the MOST difficult problem in sending an astronaut to Mars?

- (A) taking along enough food and water
- (B) the cost of such a trip
- (C) building a giant spacecraft in orbit
- (D) finding astronauts willing to be gone for more than a year

2. Choose the word that gives the BEST meaning for the underlined prefix below.

They would then <u>re</u>enter the spacecraft and blast off for the six-month return trip.

- (A) again
- (B) before
- (C) not
- (D) out

3. Choose the word that means the OPPOSITE of the underlined word.

. . . the astronauts will be <u>exposed</u> to dangerous solar winds . . .

- (A) opened
- (B) protected
- (C) hidden
- (D) explained

4. Choose the word that has NEARLY the same meaning as the underlined word.

In 1989, scientists <u>proposed</u> building a giant spacecraft in orbit.

- (A) suggested
- (B) denied
- (C) introduced
- (D) rejected

Correct answers are on page 122.

Americans read about President Richard Nixon's resignation.

CHAPTER 13

Watergate

Reading Skill: Separating Facts from Opinions

Expand Your Vocabulary: The U.S. Constitution

Get Ready to Read

1. Should the president have to obey the same laws as everyone else? Why or why not? Meet in groups of three or four and share your ideas.

____

____

____

2. Read the first two paragraphs of the reading selection on the next page. What do you think the Watergate chapter will discuss? What do you think the final result of Watergate was?

____

____

____

Watergate

1 In the United States, the president shares power with Congress and the courts. The Constitution gives the House of Representatives the power to say when it thinks the president has committed a crime. Then the Senate must have a trial. If the Senate decides that the president is guilty, he is removed from the
5 presidency. The vice president then becomes president. This power to remove a president was tested in 1974.

On the morning of June 17, 1972, five men were caught while they were breaking into the Watergate Hotel in Washington, D.C. Inside the building was an office of the Democratic Party, one of the two main political parties in the
10 United States. These **burglars** appeared to be spying on the Democrats. The FBI learned that the Watergate burglars were hired by people working for the Republican Party. These people wanted President Richard Nixon to be reelected.

President Nixon knew that if people learned about this crime it would cause a **scandal**. As a result, he might not be reelected. So he ordered the FBI to
15 stop **investigating** the burglary. President Nixon said he was trying to protect the nation. That was a lie. The president was using his power to protect his friends. This was a serious crime.

President Nixon makes his last speech before quitting his job as president on August 19, 1974.

At first the plan seemed to work. President Nixon was easily reelected. Some reporters, however, still thought he was somehow connected to the burglary. The Senate decided to investigate. One burglar told the Senate committee that President Nixon's advisers planned the crime. President Nixon fired the advisers. In a television speech, he said he did not know about the burglary or any plans to keep it secret.

Millions of Americans watched the Senate investigation on television. One man who worked for the president shocked the committee. He **testified** that all the president's meetings and phone calls were recorded. These recordings would either prove or disprove the president's guilt. The president, however, refused to give up the tapes. The Supreme Court then ordered him to give Congress the tapes. The president's actions and the tapes made most people in Congress sure that he was guilty of a crime.

After a long, difficult discussion, a House committee **recommended** that the Senate put the president on trial for hiding a crime. It seemed certain that the House would take the committee's advice and that the Senate would find him guilty. On August 9, 1974, President Nixon **resigned** rather than wait for Congress to force him to leave. Vice President Gerald Ford became president. President Ford quickly told the country, "Our Constitution works. Our great republic is a government of laws, not of men."

Check Your Understanding

1. What kind of building is the Watergate?

____

____

2. Why did the Senate want the recordings of the president's meetings and phone calls?

____

____

3. What did President Gerald Ford mean when he said, "Our great republic is a government of laws, not of men"?

____

____

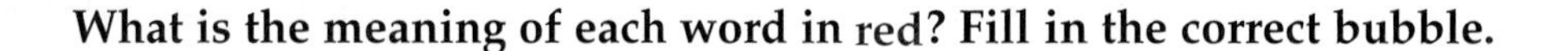

Build Your Vocabulary

What is the meaning of each word in red? Fill in the correct bubble.

1. Five men were caught while they were breaking into the Watergate Hotel . . . These **burglars** appeared to be spying on the Democrats.

   Ⓐ people who live in an apartment
   Ⓑ members of a political group
   Ⓒ people who break into buildings to steal things
   Ⓓ government officials

2. President Nixon knew that if people learned about this crime it would cause a **scandal**. As a result, he might not be reelected.

   Ⓐ public shock when someone important does something wrong
   Ⓑ accident
   Ⓒ confusion about what has happened
   Ⓓ crisis

3. As a result, he might not be reelected. So he ordered the FBI to stop **investigating** the burglary.

   Ⓐ talking about something
   Ⓑ trying to find information about something
   Ⓒ hiding something
   Ⓓ lying about something

4. One man who worked for the president shocked the committee. He **testified** that all the president's meetings and phone calls were recorded.

   Ⓐ refused to say
   Ⓑ recommended
   Ⓒ formally told an official or court
   Ⓓ did not agree

5. After a long, difficult discussion, a House committee **recommended** that the Senate put the president on trial for hiding a crime. It seemed certain that the House would take the committee's advice and that the Senate would find him guilty.

   Ⓐ suggested strongly that an idea was good
   Ⓑ said quietly
   Ⓒ refused to say what to do
   Ⓓ wrote a law

6. On August 9, 1974, President Nixon **resigned** rather than wait for Congress to force him to leave.

   Ⓐ quit his job
   Ⓑ ran for reelection
   Ⓒ said he was guilty
   Ⓓ recorded a speech

Separating Facts from Opinions

A *fact* is something that you can prove. An *opinion* is someone's idea or belief that cannot be proved. You can agree or disagree with an opinion. Opinions often use words such as *good, bad, best, worst,* and *too.*

Fact: President Nixon resigned on August 9, 1974.

Opinion: President Nixon was not a very good president.

Fact or Opinion? Fill in the correct bubble.

	Fact	Opinion
1. The U.S. Constitution is too hard to understand.	Ⓕ	Ⓞ
2. In 1972, the Democratic Party had offices in the Watergate Hotel.	Ⓕ	Ⓞ
3. The U.S. Constitution gives Congress the power to remove a president from office.	Ⓕ	Ⓞ
4. Watergate is the worst scandal in American history.	Ⓕ	Ⓞ
5. President Richard Nixon was re-elected to the presidency in 1972.	Ⓕ	Ⓞ
6. The Supreme Court ordered President Nixon to give Congress the recordings of his meetings and phone calls.	Ⓕ	Ⓞ
7. Recording meetings and phone calls is a bad idea.	Ⓕ	Ⓞ
8. President Nixon's decision to resign was good for the United States.	Ⓕ	Ⓞ
9. After President Nixon resigned, Vice President Ford became president.	Ⓕ	Ⓞ
10. President Ford was a better president than President Nixon was.	Ⓕ	Ⓞ

Expand Your Vocabulary

The U.S. Constitution

Read the definitions below of four words that are related to the U.S. Constitution.

impeach /ɪmˈpitʃ/ *verb* to say officially that a person in government is probably guilty of a crime (Only Congress can impeach the president.)

The House of Representatives voted to impeach the president.

repeal /rɪˈpil/ *verb* to cancel or get rid of a law

In 1933, Congress voted to repeal the Eighteenth Amendment.

term /tɜrm/ *noun* the amount of time a person has an elected job

U.S. senators are elected to a six-year term.

veto /ˈvitoʊ/ *verb* to refuse to sign a bill, and stop it from becoming a law (Only the president can veto a bill that Congress passes.)

The president told Congress he would veto any bill that increased taxes.

Fill in each blank with the correct word from above.

1. The mayor thought it was time for a change. She therefore decided not to run for another ______________________.
2. A president must also obey the laws. If he doesn't, the House of Representatives can ______________________ him.
3. One of the president's important powers is his ability to ______________________ a bill even if Congress approves it.
4. Many citizens thought the new law was unfair to them. They wanted their representatives to work to ______________________ it.

Put It in Writing

Write a letter to an elected official. It might be one in your town or city or a representative in Washington, D.C. Ask the official to work for or against a law. Try to use one or more of the words above.

A child touches the name of a soldier killed in Vietnam at the Vietnam Memorial in Washington, D.C.

CHAPTER 14

Remembering the Vietnam War

Reading Skill: Summarizing

Expand Your Vocabulary: Military Abbreviations

Get Ready to Read

1. Does your city or community have a statue of a famous person? Does it have a bridge, park, or street named for someone? What is the reason for making or building these things?

____

____

____

2. Look at the picture above and read the title of this chapter. What information do you predict will be included in this chapter?

____

____

____

Remembering the Vietnam War

1 Through much of the 1960s and into the 1970s, the United States fought a bloody war in Southeast Asia. U.S. troops were sent to Vietnam to fight communism. But some Americans felt this only helped an unfair and **corrupt** government. Other Americans felt strongly that the United States had to stop 5 communism in Vietnam. They were afraid nearby countries might also become communist.

As U.S. soldiers were killed, more Americans began to wonder if the war 10 was right. **Opponents** of the war had huge rallies. They often fought with angry supporters of the war. After years of hard 15 fighting, the United States was no closer to winning the war. President Richard Nixon decided to bring the U.S. troops home from 20 Vietnam. On March 29, 1973, the last U.S. troops came home, but Americans didn't welcome them with parades and treat them as heroes.

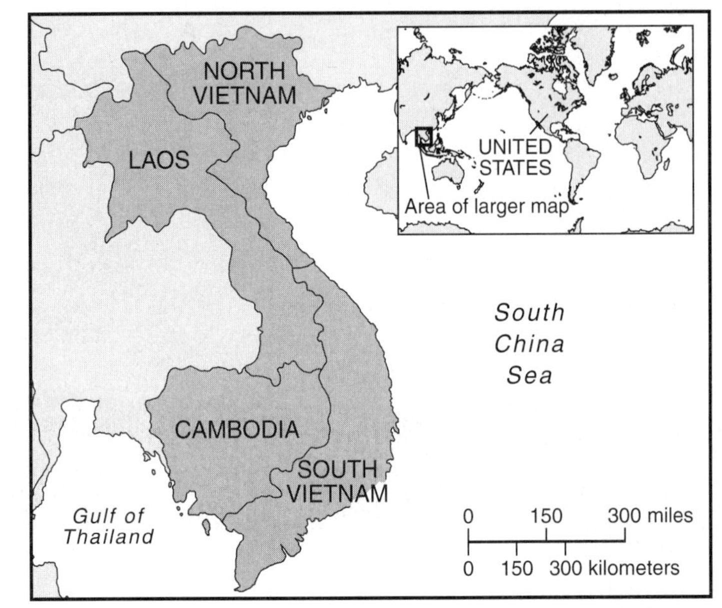

Vietnam is across the Pacific Ocean from the United States.

Americans were still sad, upset, and angry with each other. In 1979, 25 a group of Vietnam **veterans** wanted to help the country feel better again. They decided that the country needed a **memorial** to honor the dead and missing Americans from the Vietnam War. By honoring the soldiers' **sacrifices**, perhaps the nation could begin to heal. The veterans decided to hold a contest to find the best design for the memorial. They received over 30 1,500 designs, including some from world-famous designers. One design seemed different from the others, however. It came from a 21-year-old college student named Maya Ying Lin, the daughter of Chinese immigrants.

At first, Lin's design shocked some people. Other memorials were white and stood above the ground. They usually included a large statue. Lin's 35 memorial was made of two black stone walls. Instead of rising aboveground, they were cut into the ground and faced each other at a slight angle. The walls were about 10 feet tall where they joined. From there, each wall **sloped** slowly

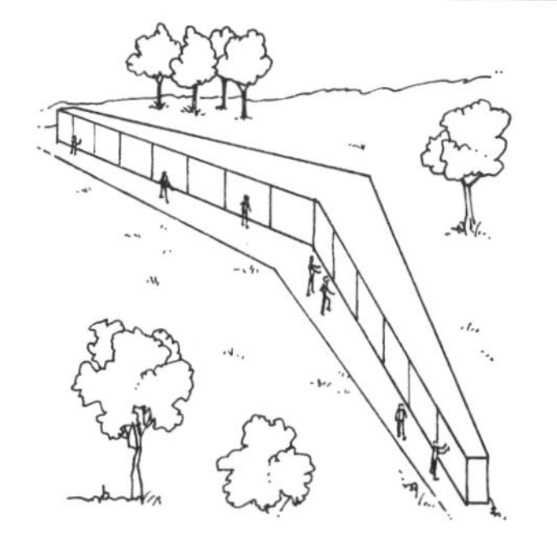

until it almost reached the ground. The names of the 58,209 people killed or missing in Vietnam were cut into the wall. They were listed in the order in which they died. All the judges voted for Lin's design.

In 1982, the memorial opened in Washington, D.C. Visitors saw the trees and sky reflected on the shiny black wall. Many people reached out and touched the names or left flowers or other items at the wall. The nation was beginning to come together again.

Today, the Vietnam Memorial is the most visited memorial in the nation. At the end of each day, park rangers collect the things left at the wall and take them to the National Museum of American History. Some are put on display there each day.

Maya Ying Lin with her winning design for the Vietnam Memorial

Check Your Understanding

1. Why did the United States send troops to Vietnam? Why were some people against doing this?

____

____

____

2. Where is the Vietnam Memorial?

____

3. Why do you think people touch the names on the wall and leave things beside it?

____

____

____

Build Your Vocabulary

What is the meaning of each word in red? Fill in the correct bubble.

1. The troops were sent to Vietnam to fight communism. But some Americans felt this only helped an unfair and **corrupt** government.

Ⓐ well-liked
Ⓑ friendly
Ⓒ dishonest
Ⓓ high-priced

2. As U.S. soldiers were killed, more Americans began to wonder if the war was right. **Opponents** of the war had huge rallies. They often fought with angry supporters of the war.

Ⓐ people who are fighting against something
Ⓑ troops who are fighting a war
Ⓒ military leaders
Ⓓ government officials

3. In 1979, a group of Vietnam **veterans** wanted to help the country feel better again.

Ⓐ Americans living in a foreign country
Ⓑ people who used to be in the military
Ⓒ leaders of a friendly government
Ⓓ people who fought against their own country

4. They decided that the country needed a **memorial** to honor the dead and missing Americans from the Vietnam War.

Ⓐ something to remind people of a person or event
Ⓑ organization of people against war
Ⓒ law that is passed by Congress and signed by the president
Ⓓ part of Washington, D.C.

5. They decided that the country needed a memorial to honor the dead and missing Americans from the Vietnam War. By honoring the soldiers' **sacrifices**, perhaps the nation could begin to heal.

Ⓐ gifts
Ⓑ disagreements
Ⓒ things that you lose or give up
Ⓓ friends and loved ones

6. The walls were about 10 feet tall where they joined. From there, each wall **sloped** slowly until it almost reached the ground.

Ⓐ made a circle
Ⓑ broke apart
Ⓒ disappeared
Ⓓ was higher at one end

Summarizing

When you *summarize* a paragraph, you start by picking out the most important part or parts. This helps you to decide what is important and to remember it later.

Read these paragraphs from the reading selection. Then answer the question that follows each paragraph.

As U.S. soldiers were killed, more Americans began to wonder if the war was right. Opponents of the war had huge rallies. They often fought with angry supporters of the war. After years of hard fighting, the United States was no closer to winning the war. President Richard Nixon decided to bring the U.S. troops home from Vietnam. On March 29, 1973, the last U.S. troops came home, but Americans didn't welcome them with parades and treat them as heroes.

1. Fill in the bubble of the sentence that BEST summarizes the paragraph.

Ⓐ President Richard Nixon was a great American president because he ended the war.

Ⓑ Many people do not like wars because they kill many soldiers.

Ⓒ Because many Americans did not like the war, they did not treat the returning soldiers as heroes.

Ⓓ American soldiers came home because they were losing the war.

At first, Lin's design shocked some people. Other memorials were white and stood above the ground. They usually included a large statue. Lin's memorial was made of two black stone walls. Instead of rising aboveground, they were cut into the ground and faced each other at a slight angle. The walls were about 10 feet tall where they joined. From there, each wall sloped slowly until it almost reached the ground. The names of the 58,209 people killed or missing in Vietnam were cut into the wall. They were listed in the order in which they died. All the judges voted for Lin's design.

2. Fill in the bubble of the sentence that BEST summarizes the paragraph.

Ⓐ Lin's unusual design surprised people, but pleased the judges.

Ⓑ The Vietnam Memorial helps people remember the war.

Ⓒ The judges did not like white memorials that stood above the ground.

Ⓓ The design for the Vietnam Memorial was chosen through a contest.

Expand Your Vocabulary

Military Abbreviations

Read the definitions below of four words that are related to men and women in wartime.

AWOL /ˈeɪˌwɔl/ *adjective* (abbreviation for *absent without leave*) gone without permission, for example, from an army base

The soldier was punished for being AWOL.

GI /ˌdʒiˈaɪ/ *noun* (abbreviation for *government issue*) a member of the army, navy, or other military service

The movie star did a show for the GIs on the air force base.

MIA /ˌɛm aɪ ˈeɪ/ *noun* (abbreviation for *missing in action*) a member of the military who is missing after a battle

After the treaty, the army began searching for the MIAs.

POW /ˌpi oʊ ˈdʌbəlju/ *noun* (abbreviation for *prisoner of war*) a person held by an enemy during a war

The POW was released to show the government's desire for peace.

True or False? Use the definitions. Fill in the correct bubble.

	True	False
1. An MIA could be a POW.	Ⓣ	Ⓕ
2. GIs that are AWOL are honored as heroes.	Ⓣ	Ⓕ
3. If a soldier surrenders to the enemy, he or she will probably become a POW.	Ⓣ	Ⓕ
4. Fear of battle might make a soldier become AWOL.	Ⓣ	Ⓕ

Put It in Writing

Write a list of questions. Imagine that you are a reporter for a newspaper. You have been assigned to report on an important battle our troops just fought. Write at least four questions you want to ask the commander after the battle. Try to use one or more of the words above.

Idioms

An *idiom* is a phrase or group of words with a special meaning. Knowing the meaning of each word will not help you understand the meaning of the phrase. Sometimes the words before and after an idiom will help you learn its meaning. Idioms are used mainly in informal conversations.

Idiom: The mayor was sorry he made such a foolish off-the-cuff statement.

Meaning: The mayor was sorry he made such a foolish unplanned statement.

Decide on the meaning of each underlined idiom. Fill in the correct bubble.

1. When you told me I had won the award, I didn't believe you at first. I was sure you were pulling my leg.

Ⓐ grabbing my foot
Ⓑ helping a friend
Ⓒ playing a joke
Ⓓ laughing out loud

2. After losing the first six games of the season, some players were ready to throw in the towel.

Ⓐ give up
Ⓑ go to the showers
Ⓒ play another sport
Ⓓ practice longer

3. For weeks, Joe bragged about how smart he was. But after he failed the exam, he had to eat his words.

Ⓐ eat lunch by himself
Ⓑ feel foolish about what he said
Ⓒ take the exam again
Ⓓ brag even more

4. Just thinking about giving a speech to the whole school gave me butterflies in my stomach.

Ⓐ made me upset and nervous
Ⓑ made me think of animals
Ⓒ made me hungry
Ⓓ made me proud

Write what you think the meaning of the underlined idiom is in each sentence.

5. After nearly failing the test, Justin decided to turn over a new leaf and start paying attention in class.

____

6. I've been down in the dumps ever since my best friend moved away.

____

7. My brother played his stereo so loud I couldn't read my homework. I finally told him to cut it out.

____

8. Even with talent and hard work, it is not easy to make it as a professional football player.

____

9. I was tickled pink to hear the class would be taking a field trip to New York City.

____

10. I was walking home at night in the dark. Then I heard a strange noise, and my hair stood on end.

____

11. Meg's science project is terrific. She should win first prize hands down.

____

12. Jason never seems to listen to his father's advice. The words just go in one ear and out the other.

____

CHAPTER

Happy Berliners tear down the Berlin Wall in November 1989.

The End of the Cold War

Reading Skill:
Summarizing

Expand Your Vocabulary:
The Free Enterprise System

Get Ready to Read

1. Study the photograph above. Why do you think people are destroying this wall?

____

____

____

2. What do you think a cold war is? How is it fought? How does it end?

____

____

The End of the Cold War

After Germany surrendered in World War II, a new kind of war began—a Cold War. It was not fought with guns and bombs. Instead it was fought with threats and angry words. The Soviet Union was on one side. It wanted to spread communism. The United States was on the other side. It wanted to **preserve** freedom, democracy, and the free enterprise system. This economic system allows people to own property and businesses.

After World War II, Germany and its capital, Berlin, were divided. The Soviet Union took over East Germany and East Berlin. The United States and its allies controlled West Germany and West Berlin. In Berlin, communism and democracy existed side by side. Conflict seemed unavoidable.

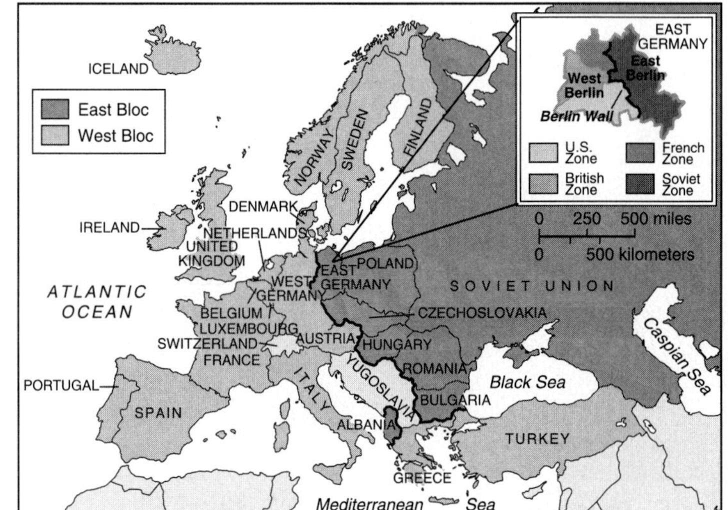

Europe after World War II

In communist East Berlin the government controlled all property and industry. Food and other necessities were difficult to get, and the people had little money to buy the things that were available. No one was allowed to **criticize** the government. Almost immediately hundreds of people began to leave East Berlin to go to West Berlin.

The communist government was **embarrassed**. On the night of August 14, 1961, East German troops began building a wall between East and West Berlin. The next day, soldiers were guarding the wall. They were told to shoot anyone who tried to reach West Berlin.

The wall, however, did not stop people from trying to escape. A few people were still able to reach West Berlin, but more than 200 did not make it and were killed. **Tensions** between the United States and Soviet Union got worse each time someone tried to escape. The Berlin Wall became a **symbol** of the Cold War.

After years of Soviet **oppression**, workers in communist countries began holding protests and strikes. In 1980, shipyard workers in communist Poland demanded a union and free elections. Officials arrested the leaders, but the strikes continued. Finally, the Polish government agreed to hold elections. In other countries people were demanding changes. As a result, they were getting more democratic governments. Even in the Soviet Union, new leaders realized they had to give people more control of their government.

Communist leaders in East Germany and East Berlin fought against change, but they too had to give in to protests and strikes. Freedom came slowly, but on November 9, 1989, the East German government was forced to open its border with West Berlin. Cheering crowds from East and West Berlin climbed the wall. Many people swung hammers to break it apart. Within days, the wall was gone. The following year, East Germany had free elections. East Germany and West Germany became one country again, and East Berlin and West Berlin became one city. The Cold War was over.

A woman escapes through a window from East Berlin to West Berlin after the Wall is built in 1961.

Check Your Understanding

1. How were Germany and Berlin divided after World War II?

2. Why did so many people risk being killed to escape from East Berlin?

3. What made Berlin an important place during the Cold War?

Build Your Vocabulary

What is the meaning of each word in red? Fill in the correct bubble.

1. The Soviet Union was on one side. It wanted to spread communism. The United States was on the other side. It wanted to **preserve** freedom, democracy, and the free enterprise system.

Ⓐ change
Ⓑ protect and keep
Ⓒ replace
Ⓓ delay or end

2. No one was allowed to **criticize** the government. Almost immediately hundreds of people began to leave East Berlin to go to West Berlin.

Ⓐ say bad things about something
Ⓑ join something
Ⓒ study certain parts of something
Ⓓ change something

3. Almost immediately hundreds of people began to leave East Berlin to go to West Berlin. The communist government was **embarrassed**.

Ⓐ quickly destroyed
Ⓑ stronger
Ⓒ hidden from the world
Ⓓ feeling foolish

4. **Tensions** between the United States and Soviet Union got worse each time someone tried to escape.

Ⓐ unfriendly feelings
Ⓑ agreements
Ⓒ walls surrounding a city
Ⓓ written messages

5. The Berlin Wall became a **symbol** of the Cold War.

Ⓐ place where something starts
Ⓑ military camp
Ⓒ something that represents something else
Ⓓ the cause of a problem

6. After years of Soviet **oppression**, workers in communist countries began holding protests and strikes.

Ⓐ chances to make money
Ⓑ promises
Ⓒ freedom
Ⓓ cruel, unfair treatment

Summarizing

When you *summarize* a paragraph, you first pick out the most important part or parts. This helps you to decide what is important and to remember it later. Then you say or write this in your own words.

1. Read the following paragraph. Then write one sentence to summarize the paragraph.

> In communist East Berlin the government controlled all property and industry. Food and other necessities were difficult to get, and the people had little money to buy the things that were available. No one was allowed to criticize the government. Almost immediately hundreds of people began to leave East Berlin to go to West Berlin.

____

____

____

2. Read the following paragraph. Then write one sentence to summarize the paragraph.

> After years of Soviet oppression, workers in communist countries began holding protests and strikes. In 1980, shipyard workers in communist Poland demanded a union and free elections. Officials arrested the leaders, but the strikes continued. Finally, the Polish government agreed to hold elections. In other countries people were demanding changes. As a result, they were getting more democratic governments. Even in the Soviet Union, new leaders realized they had to give people more control of their government.

____

____

____

Expand Your Vocabulary

The Free Enterprise System

Read the definitions below of four words that are related to the free enterprise system.

corporation /kɔrpəˈreɪʃən/ *noun* a large or small group of people legally allowed to do business as a single organization

My brothers formed a corporation that makes and sells furniture.

credit /ˈkrɛdɪt/ *noun* a system for buying things and paying for them later, usually with an added cost

If we buy a car on credit, we can take four years to pay for it.

dividend /ˈdɪvɪˌdɛnd/ *noun* money that is earned by a company and given to the owners

The computer company usually pays a dividend twice a year.

revenue /ˈrɛvəˌnu/ *noun* money that a business earns, or taxes that the government collects

Hotels near the beach lost much revenue because of the bad weather.

True or False? Use the definitions. Fill in the correct bubble.

	True	False
1. If a store sells you a stove on credit, you will pay less for it.	Ⓣ	Ⓕ
2. The more things a store sells the more revenue it will have that year.	Ⓣ	Ⓕ
3. Three people cannot become a corporation.	Ⓣ	Ⓕ
4. A corporation with a lot of revenue will probably pay a dividend.	Ⓣ	Ⓕ

Put It in Writing

Write a description of a business you would like to own. Tell how it will make money for you. Try to use one or more of the words above.

CHAPTER

Smoke comes out of the World Trade Center in New York after terrorists fly two planes into it.

The Attack on the World Trade Center

Reading Skill:
Making Inferences

Expand Your Vocabulary:
Terrorism and International Conflicts

Get Ready to Read

1. Look at the picture above and read the title of this chapter. List three things you know about this event.

____

____

____

2. What do you think you will learn as you read this chapter?

____

____

____

The Attack on the World Trade Center

September 11, 2001, has been called the day that changed everything. On that day terrorists took control of four large planes. They crashed two planes into the World Trade Center, New York City's two tallest buildings. Both buildings **collapsed** in flames. The third plane hit the Pentagon, the main offices of the U.S. military, in Arlington, Virginia, near Washington, D.C. The passengers of the fourth plane fought the terrorists. Instead of hitting another building, the plane crashed in a field.

Nearly 3,000 people died in the World Trade Center. The dead included hundreds of rescue workers. More than 100 people were killed in the Pentagon. All 266 passengers on the four planes were killed.

Before September 11, people in the United States felt safe at home. Two oceans helped keep enemies far from its shores. Powerful weapons and a strong military protected its borders. That feeling of **security** was lost on that September day.

The United States now had a new kind of enemy. Attacks on citizens or important places would be difficult to stop. There seemed to be no way to guard every important bridge or building.

The United States has encountered many **challenges** throughout its history. Somehow, it has been successful each time. And each time, the nation grew stronger. After the **tragedy** of September 11, people began coming together almost immediately. Thousands of people gave blood and millions of dollars to help the victims and their families. Americans flew flags to show their love for their country. The mayor of New York visited the ruins to praise and encourage the workers.

An American flag hangs over rescuers in the ruins of the World Trade Center.

President George W. Bush **assured** the nation that it was strong and was going to win the war on terrorism.

Government officials began searching for anyone connected to the terrorist attack. Within days, they learned that Osama bin Laden, a man with extreme religious beliefs, planned the attack. So U.S. and British troops went into Afghanistan and attacked his terrorist training camps there. The president then created the Office of Homeland Security. This important department **coordinates** the work of several groups to protect America. The president warned this was going to be the start of a long and difficult fight.

New York City began to plan for a new World Trade Center. On February 27, 2003, New York state officials decided on a building 1,776 feet (541 meters) high. In the plans, it is 400 feet (122 meters) higher than the original World Trade Center. It also includes a memorial to honor the people killed on September 11.

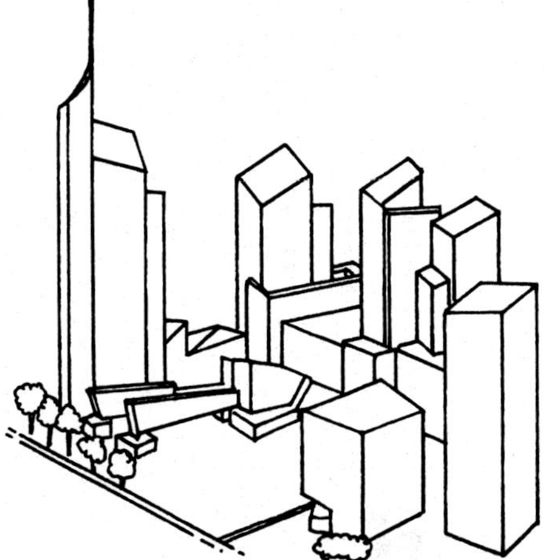

The design for the new World Trade Center

Check Your Understanding

1. How many planes were used in the terrorist attack of September 11, 2001?

2. List two things people did to support the victims and the nation after the terrorist attack.

3. September 11, 2001, is sometimes called the day that changed everything. What are some of the things that changed?

Build Your Vocabulary

What is the meaning of each word in red? Fill in the correct bubble.

1. They crashed two planes into the World Trade Center, New York City's two tallest buildings. Both buildings **collapsed** in flames.

   Ⓐ joined
   Ⓑ exploded
   Ⓒ disappeared
   Ⓓ fell down

2. Two oceans helped keep enemies far from its shores. Powerful weapons and a strong military protected its borders. That feeling of **security** was lost on that September day.

   Ⓐ safety
   Ⓑ danger
   Ⓒ power
   Ⓓ freedom

3. The United States has encountered many **challenges** throughout its history. Somehow, it has been successful each time.

   Ⓐ surprises
   Ⓑ terrible defeats in wars
   Ⓒ accidents
   Ⓓ difficult problems

4. After the **tragedy** of September 11, people began coming together almost immediately.

   Ⓐ important meeting
   Ⓑ very bad event that involves death
   Ⓒ news
   Ⓓ actions that show your love for your country

5. President George W. Bush **assured** the nation that it was strong and was going to win the war on terrorism.

   Ⓐ warned
   Ⓑ said firmly
   Ⓒ frightened
   Ⓓ attacked

6. This important department **coordinates** the work of several groups to protect America.

   Ⓐ gets rid of something
   Ⓑ finds a job for someone
   Ⓒ makes things work together
   Ⓓ makes something much larger

Making Inferences

You can sometimes use facts that are stated directly to guess certain facts that are not stated. This is called *making inferences*. Making inferences helps you understand more of what you read.

Stated Fact: Terrorists took control of four large planes. They crashed two planes into the World Trade Center.

Inference: The terrorists knew how to fly large planes.

Fill in the bubble of the most likely inference that you can make from each of these stated facts.

1. The passengers of the fourth plane fought the terrorists. Instead of hitting another building, the plane crashed in a field.

   Ⓐ The passengers knew how to fly a large plane.
   Ⓑ The passengers stopped the terrorists from hitting a building.
   Ⓒ The fourth plane had more passengers.
   Ⓓ The fourth plane was smaller than the others were.

2. Nearly 3,000 people died in the World Trade Center. The dead included hundreds of rescue workers.

   Ⓐ Rescue workers are not well trained.
   Ⓑ The rescue workers were able to save some people.
   Ⓒ Rescue workers got into the building before it collapsed.
   Ⓓ No one in the World Trade Center survived.

3. After the tragedy of September 11, people began coming together almost immediately. . . . The mayor of New York visited the ruins to praise and encourage the workers.

   Ⓐ The mayor once worked at the World Trade Center.
   Ⓑ It will take a long time to rebuild the World Trade Center.
   Ⓒ The workers were not doing a very good job.
   Ⓓ Work at the ruins began very quickly.

4. Within days, the government learned that Osama bin Laden had planned the attacks. U.S. and British troops went into Afghanistan and attacked his training camps.

   Ⓐ There will be no more attacks in the future.
   Ⓑ Osama bin Laden rules Afghanistan.
   Ⓒ The terrorists did not act alone. They had help.
   Ⓓ There will be more attacks in the future.

Expand Your Vocabulary

Terrorism and International Conflicts

Read the definitions below of four words that are related to terrorism and international conflicts.

coalition /koʊəˈlɪʃən/ *noun* a group of nations joined together for some special purpose, such as fighting against terrorism

Soldiers from the coalition surrounded the terrorist training camp.

evacuate /ɪˈvækjuˌeɪt/ *verb* to leave a particular area to avoid danger

The teachers and the children evacuated the school as soon as they heard the fire alarm.

hijack /ˈhaɪˌdʒæk/ *verb* to take control of a moving vehicle, such as an airplane or automobile, by force or violence

The attempt to hijack the airplane was stopped by a security guard.

sanctions /ˈsænkʃənz/ *noun* economic or political actions taken by several nations to punish another nation

Because of the U.S. sanctions, businesses were not allowed to sell computers to the communist government.

Fill in each blank with the correct word from above.

1. United States and England formed a(n) ______________________ in the war with Iraq.
2. People boarding an airplane may not carry anything that might be used to ______________________ the plane.
3. Instead of attacking the cruel dictatorship, several nations decided to use ______________________.
4. People were told to ______________________ the building because there might be a bomb there.

Put It in Writing

Write a paragraph about an important problem that the United States needs to solve today. Try to use one or more of the words above.

Vocabulary Tests

One type of vocabulary test asks you to choose a word that completes two different sentences. The correct answer is often a word with more than one meaning. One meaning is needed to complete the first sentence, and a second meaning is needed to complete the second sentence. Sometimes the correct answer is used in very different ways in the two sentences. When taking this kind of test, you must think of all the possible meanings and uses for each word choice. Sometimes tests will try to trick you by including words that look or sound like the correct answer, but are wrong.

Practice this strategy on these sample questions.

Directions: Which word best completes BOTH sentences?

S1. Marge's red shoes ________________ her hat.

I will need a ________________ to start the campfire.

drink	yard	goal	match
(A)	(B)	(C)	(D)

S2. I left my ________________ at school, so I was locked out of the house.

We must fix the ________________ on the old piano.

keys	work	legs	notes
(A)	(B)	(C)	(D)

Did you think of all the meanings of the words before choosing your answers?
The correct answers are on page 122.

PRACTICE TEST

Directions: Which word best completes BOTH sentences?

1. The captain was afraid that the storm would ________________ his ship.

   Fill the ________________ with soap and water and wash the dishes.

lift	link	pan	sink
(A)	(B)	(C)	(D)

2. We saw an alligator sleeping on the ________________ of the river.

   I hope the ________________ will lend me the money I need.

side	band	bank	sand
(A)	(B)	(C)	(D)

3. A boy in my class has a bad ________________ of the flu.

   Jay put his guitar in a black leather ________________.

bag	case	carry	place
(A)	(B)	(C)	(D)

4. The workers presented several ________________ to their boss.

   Our principal ________________ that students arrive on time for class.

requires	demands	declines	asks
(A)	(B)	(C)	(D)

5. Please ________________ your flashlight in my direction.

   This hill is the highest ________________ in the entire county.

show	height	point	move
(A)	(B)	(C)	(D)

6. I love getting long ________________ from my friends in Kansas.

   The names were written in large ________________ on the chalkboard.

letters	messages	marks	signs
(A)	(B)	(C)	(D)

Correct answers are on page 122.

Glossary

Pronunciation Key											
Consonants						Vowels					
p	pot	θ	thing	h	hot	i	beat	ʊ	book		
b	ball	ð	that	m	map	ɪ	bit	u	boot		
t	tall	s	see	n	not	eɪ	late	ʌ	cut		
d	dog	z	zoo	ŋ	sing	ɛ	let	ə	about		
k	cat	ʃ	shop	w	well	æ	pat	ɜ	bird		
g	go	ʒ	measure	r	ride	ɑ	pot	aɪ	why		
f	fine	tʃ	chip	l	look	ɔ	caught	aʊ	how		
v	voice	dʒ	jump	j	you	oʊ	coat	ɔɪ	toy		

The symbol /ˈ/ before a syllable means that it is the main stressed syllable in a word.

The symbol /ˌ/ before a syllable means that it is the second most important stressed syllable.

The **red** numbers tell which chapter each word is taught in.

activist /ˈæktɪvɪst/ *noun* a person who tries to change things through protests, strikes, or other actions **(9)**

adviser /ædˈvaɪzər/ *noun* a person who helps someone make a decision **(10)**

alliance /əˈlaɪəns/ *noun* an agreement between two or more countries to help each other **(10)**

ally /ˈæˌlaɪ/ *noun* a country that joins another country for a purpose, such as fighting a war **(8)**

ambassador /æmˈbæsədər/ *noun* an official who represents a government in another country **(8)**

amendment /əˈmɛndmənt/ *noun* a change **(4)**

angle /ˈæŋgəl/ *noun* the shape or space created by two straight lines that touch or cross each other **(2)**

appliance /əˈplaɪəns/ *noun* a small machine that does work in the house **(5)**

application /æplɪˈkeɪʃən/ *noun* a form that you write on to ask for something **(1)**

artificial /ˌɑrtɪˈfɪʃəl/ *adjective* unnatural **(6)**

assassinate /əˈsæsɪˌneɪt/ *verb* to kill someone important **(11)**

assure /əˈʃɜr/ *verb* to say firmly that something is true **(16)**

AWOL /ˈeɪˌwɔl/ *adjective* abbreviation for Absent Without Leave; gone without permission, for example, from an army base **(14)**

background /ˈbækˌgraund/ *noun* your past and present life **(6)**

bankrupt /ˈbæŋkˌrʌpt/ *adjective* unable to pay what you owe and continue doing business **(5)**

blockade /blɑˈkeɪd/ *noun* an action of using military force to stop supplies from entering or leaving a place **(10)**

boycott /ˈbɔɪˌkɑt/ *noun* an action of refusing to buy or use something **(9)**

burglar /ˈbɜrglər/ *noun* a person who breaks into buildings to steal things **(13)**

campaign /kæmˈpeɪn/ *noun* a series of actions done by a person or group of people to reach a goal, such as winning an election **(4)**

candidate /ˈkændɪdˌdeɪt/ *noun* a person who is trying to be elected to a government job **(4)**

capitalism /ˈkæpɪtəlɪzəm/ *noun* a system in which businesses are owned by people, not the government **(9)**

challenge /ˈtʃæləndʒ/ *noun* a difficult problem that you have to deal with **(16)**

civil rights /ˌsɪvɪl ˈraɪts/ *noun* the freedoms that everyone in society should have **(11)**

coalition /koʊəˈlɪʃən/ *noun* a group of nations joined together for some special purpose, such as fighting against terrorism **(16)**

collapse /kəˈlæps/ *verb* to fall down **(16)**

combination /kɑmbɪˈneɪʃən/ *noun* a set of things that are used together **(2)**

community /kəˈmjunəti/ *noun* a group of people who live together **(1)**

compromise /ˈkɑmprəˌmaɪz/ *noun* a decision in which everyone gives up part of what he or she wants **(10)**

conflict /ˈkɑnˌflɪkt/ *noun* a disagreement or fight **(10)**

congratulate /kənˈgrætʃuˌleɪt/ *verb* to tell someone you are happy about his or her achievement **(7)**

coordinate /koʊˈɔrdɪˌneɪt/ *verb* to make things work together **(16)**

corporation /kɔrpəˈreɪʃən/ *noun* a large or small group of people legally allowed to do business as a single organization **(15)**

corrupt /kəˈrʌpt/ *adjective* using power in a dishonest way **(14)**

credit /ˈkrɛdɪt/ *noun* a system for buying things and paying for them later, usually with an added cost **(15)**

crisis /ˈkraɪsɪs/ *noun* a difficult and dangerous situation **(8)**

criticize /ˈkrɪtɪˌsaɪz/ *verb* to say bad things about someone or something **(15)**

defeat /dɪˈfit/ *verb* to beat someone or something in a vote or fight **(4)**

demand /dɪˈmænd/ *noun* a strong request **(4)**

depart /dɪˈpɑrt/ *verb* to go away **(12)**

deposit /dɪˈpɑzɪt/ *noun* to put money in a bank **(6)**

desperate /ˈdɛspərət/ *adjective* needing something badly and willing to do anything to get it **(6)**

determination /dɪˌtɛrmɪˈneɪʃən/ *noun* a strong desire to continue trying **(6)**

diplomacy /dɪˈploʊməsi/ *noun* the skill to arrange agreements between nations **(10)**

disaster /dɪˈzæstər/ *noun* an event that causes a lot of damage and death **(3)**

discrimination /dɪˌskrɪmɪˈneɪʃən/ *noun* unfair treatment for a particular group of people **(11)**

disqualify /dɪsˈkwɔlɪfaɪ/ *verb* to prevent someone from doing something because of a rule **(1)**

dividend /ˈdɪvɪˌdɛnd/ *noun* money that is earned by a company and given to the owners **(15)**

embarrassed /ɪmˈbærəst/ *adjective* feeling foolish **(15)**

encounter / ɪnˈkaʊntər/ *verb* to start having problems when you are trying to do something **(12)**

encourage /ɪnˈkɜrədʒ/ *verb* to tell someone that he or she should do something **(12)**

epidemic /ˌɛpɪˈdɛmɪk/ *noun* a disease that spreads quickly **(5)**

estimate /ˈɛstɪˌmeɪt/ *verb* to guess an amount carefully **(3)**

evacuate /ɪˈvækjuˌeɪt/ *verb* to leave a particular area to avoid danger **(16)**

experiment /ɪkˈspɛrɪmənt/ *verb* to try different things to see which works **(2)**

expire /ɪkˈspaɪr/ *verb* to stop being good or legal **(9)**

fascism /ˈfæʃɪzəm/ *noun* a type of government that completely controls people's lives, does not allow disagreement, and says that its people are better than all other people **(7)**

fatalities /fəˈtælətiz/ *noun* deaths **(2)**

fault /fɔlt/ *noun* a large crack in the Earth's surface **(3)**

foreign /ˈfɔrən/ *adjective* in or from another country **(8)**

fringe benefit /ˌfrɪndʒ ˈbɛnəfɪt/ *noun* something, such as medical care, that is given to a worker in addition to his or her pay **(9)**

genocide /ˈdʒɛnəˌsaɪd/ *noun* the planned killing of an entire race or culture **(7)**

geology /dʒiˈɑlədʒi/ *noun* the scientific study of the Earth and the rocks and soil it is made of **(3)**

ghetto /ˈgɛtoʊ/ *noun* a part of a city in which a specific group of people is forced to live **(7)**

GI /ˌdʒiˈaɪ/ *noun* abbreviation for Government Issue; a member of the army, navy, or other military service **(14)**

harmony /ˈhɑrməni/ *noun* a pleasant combination of two or more musical sounds **(5)**

hijack /ˈhaɪˌdʒæk/ *verb* to take control of a moving vehicle, such as an airplane or automobile, by force or violence **(16)**

horizontal /hɔrɪˈzɑntəl/ *adjective* flat and level like the line where earth and sky meet **(2)**

hostile /ˈhɑstəl/ *adjective* very unfriendly **(10)**

impeach /ɪmˈpitʃ/ *verb* to say officially that a person in government is probably guilty of a crime. Only Congress can impeach the president. **(13)**

inferior /ɪnˈfɪriər/ *adjective* worse **(7)**

inflation /ɪnˈfleɪʃən/ *noun* the continuing rise of prices over time **(6)**

inspire /ɪnˈspaɪr/ *verb* to cause a strong feeling in someone **(11)**

integrate /ˈɪntəˌgreɪt/ *verb* to include all races in the same schools, jobs, housing, and other places **(11)**

interest /ˈɪntrəst/ *noun* money you pay to borrow money, or money a bank pays you for saving your money there **(6)**

investigate /ɪnˈvɛstɪˌgeɪt/ *verb* to try to find information about something **(13)**

isolated /ˈæɪsəˌleɪtɪd/ *adjective* far away from other things **(2)**

Jim Crow /ˌdʒɪm ˈkroʊ/ *noun* a system of rules or customs in the past of discriminating against African Americans **(11)**

liberate /ˈlɪbəˌreɪt/ *verb* to set someone free from prison or a government's control **(8)**

lunar /ˈlunər/ *adjective* related to the moon **(12)**

magnitude /ˈmægnəˌtud/ *noun* how powerful an earthquake is **(3)**

majority /məˈdʒɔrəti/ *noun* more than half **(4)**

memorial /məˈmɔriəl/ *noun* something to remind people of a person or event, usually a building or a statue **(14)**

MIA /ˌɛm aɪ ˈeɪ/ *noun* abbreviation for Missing in Action; a member of the military who is missing after a battle **(14)**

migrate /ˈmaɪˌgreɪt/ *verb* to move to a new place **(1)**

mission /ˈmɪʃən/ *noun* an important job that someone gives you **(12)**

navigate /ˈnævɪˌgeɪt/ *verb* to guide an object, such as a ship or airplane, to a particular place **(12)**

negotiate /nəˈgoʊʃiˌeɪt/ *verb* to discuss disagreements **(9)**

neutral /ˈnutrəl/ *adjective* not choosing sides in a war between other countries **(8)**

newcomer /ˈnukʌmər/ *noun* someone who has just arrived somewhere **(1)**

opponent /əˈpoʊnənt/ *noun* someone who is fighting against something **(14)**

oppose /əˈpoʊz/ *verb* to fight against someone or something **(10)**

oppression /əˈprɛʃən/ *noun* cruel, unfair treatment by someone with power **(15)**

orbit /ˈɔrbɪt/ *noun* the path something takes around an object in space **(12)**

order /ˈɔrdər/ *verb* to officially tell someone to do something **(11)**

parallel /ˈpærəˌlɛl/ *adjective* never crossing and always separated by the same distance **(2)**

perform /pərˈfɔrm/ *verb* to do something complicated **(12)**

POW /ˌpi oʊ ˈdʌbəlju/ *noun* abbreviation for Prisoner of War; a person held by an enemy during a war **(14)**

predict /prɪˈdɪkt/ *verb* to say what will happen in the future **(3)**

preserve /prɪˈzɛrv/ *verb* to protect and keep something **(15)**

primary election /ˌpraɪmɛri ɪˈlɛkʃən/ *noun* an early election in which voters choose a small number of people to compete in the later election **(4)**

process /ˈprɑˌsɛs/ *noun* a series of actions or events **(4)**

prohibit /proʊˈhɪbɪt/ *verb* to make something illegal **(5)**

propaganda /ˌprɑpəˈgændə/ *noun* information that is supposed to make people believe something **(7)**

prosperity /prɑˈspɛrɪti/ *noun* success and money **(6)**

protest /ˈproʊˌtɛst/ *noun* an action that shows that people don't like something **(4)**

publicize /ˈpʌbləˌsaɪz/ *verb* to give out information about something to a lot of people **(9)**

rally /ˈræli/ *noun* a large public meeting to show that people like a particular idea **(4)**

recommend /ˌrɛkəˈmɛnd/ *verb* to suggest strongly that something is good **(13)**

recruit /rɪˈkrut/ *verb* to get someone to join a group **(7)**

refuse /rɪˈfjuz/ *verb* say that you will not do something **(1)**

remarkable /rɪˈmɑrkəbəl/ *adjective* unusual and great **(5)**

repeal /rɪˈpil/ *verb* to cancel or get rid of a law **(13)**

representative /rɛprɪˈzɛntətɪv/ *noun* a person who is elected to make decisions for other people **(11)**

request /rɪˈkwɛst/ *noun* an act of asking for something **(2)**

resident /ˈrɛzɪdənt/ *noun* a person who lives in a particular place **(1)**

resign /rɪˈzaɪn/ *verb* to quit your job **(13)**

revenue /ˈrɛvəˌnu/ *noun* money that a business earns, or taxes that the government collects **(15)**

rhythm /ˈrɪðəm/ *noun* a pattern of repeated notes or beats in music **(5)**

Richter Scale /ˈrɪktər ˌskeɪl/ *noun* a system for measuring the size of an earthquake **(3)**

ruins /ˈruɪnz/ *noun* [plural] what is left after buildings are destroyed **(3)**

rural /ˈrurəl/ *adjective* related to the countryside or the people who live there **(1)**

sacrifice /ˈsækrɪˌfaɪs/ *noun* something you give up or lose in order to do something else **(14)**

sanctions /ˈsænkʃənz/ *noun* economic or political actions taken by several nations to punish another nation **(16)**

satellite /ˈsætəˌlaɪt/ *noun* a piece of equipment sent into space to go around the Earth and send back information **(12)**

scandal /ˈskændəl/ *noun* public shock when someone important does something wrong **(13)**

security /sɪˈkjʊrəti/ *noun* safety **(16)**

segregation /ˌsɛgrəˈgeɪʃən/ *noun* the practice of separating the races in schools, jobs, housing, and other places **(11)**

seniority /ˌsɪnˈjɔrəti/ *noun* the higher rank given to someone because of how long he or she has been an employee **(9)**

sensitive /ˈsɛnsətɪv/ *adjective* able to feel or measure small changes easily **(3)**

sit-in /ˈsɪtˌɪn/ *noun* a way of protesting something by sitting down as a group in a place and refusing to move **(11)**

slope /sloʊp/ *verb* to be higher at one end than the other **(14)**

solo /ˈsoʊloʊ/ *noun* one voice or musical instrument performing music alone **(5)**

solution /səˈluʃən/ *noun* an answer to a problem **(2)**

stereotype /ˈstɛriəˌtaɪp/ *noun* a belief that people have particular qualities because they are members of a particular race, sex, or culture **(7)**

strike /straɪk/ *noun* a period of time when workers stop working to protest something **(9)**

suburban /səˈbɜrbən/ *adjective* related to towns near a large city **(1)**

succeed /səkˈsid/ *verb* to do what people expected or hoped for **(12)**

superior /səˈpɪriər/ *adjective* better **(7)**

superpower /ˈsupərˌpaʊər/ *noun* a powerful nation, especially one that has nuclear weapons **(10)**

support /səˈpɔrt/ *noun* help **(7)**

surrender /səˈrɛndər/ *verb* to give up **(8)**

suspect /səˈspɛkt/ *verb* to believe that something unusual might be true, although you are not sure **(8)**

symbol /ˈsɪmbəl/ *noun* something, such as a picture, that represents something else **(15)**

tensions /ˈtɛnʃənz/ *noun* unfriendly feelings **(15)**

term /tɜrm/ *noun* the amount of time a person has an elected job **(13)**

testify /ˈtɛstəˌfaɪ/ *verb* to formally tell something to an official or court **(13)**

threaten /ˈθrɛtən/ *verb* to say that you are going to do something bad to someone else **(8)**

tragedy /ˈtrædʒədi/ *noun* a very bad event that involves death **(16)**

treaty /ˈtriti/ *noun* an agreement between two or more countries **(10)**

tremor /ˈtrɛmər/ *noun* a short shaking movement **(3)**

trio /ˈtrioʊ/ *noun* a group of three people or instruments performing music **(5)**

union /ˈjunjən/ *noun* an organization of workers **(9)**

unique /juˈnik/ *adjective* different from anything else **(5)**

unproductive /ˌʌnprəˈdʌktɪv/ *adjective* unable to bring good results **(6)**

urban /ˈɜrbən/ *adjective* related to a city **(1)**

vertical /ˈvɜrtɪkəl/ *adjective* straight up and down **(2)**

veteran /ˈvɛtrən/ *noun* someone who used to be in the military **(14)**

veto /ˈvitoʊ/ *verb* to refuse to sign a bill, and stop it from becoming a law. Only the president can veto a law that Congress passes. **(13)**

withdraw /wɪθˈdrɔ/ *verb* to take money out of a bank account **(6)**

wreckage /ˈrɛkədʒ/ *noun* parts left after something is destroyed **(8)**

States, Abbreviations, and Capitals

State	Postal Abbreviation	Capital
Alabama	AL	Montgomery
Alaska	AK	Juneau
Arizona	AZ	Phoenix
Arkansas	AR	Little Rock
California	CA	Sacramento
Colorado	CO	Denver
Connecticut	CT	Hartford
Delaware	DE	Dover
Florida	FL	Tallahassee
Georgia	GA	Atlanta
Hawaii	HI	Honolulu
Idaho	ID	Boise
Illinois	IL	Springfield
Indiana	IN	Indianapolis
Iowa	IA	Des Moines
Kansas	KS	Topeka
Kentucky	KY	Frankfort
Louisiana	LA	Baton Rouge
Maine	ME	Augusta
Maryland	MD	Annapolis
Massachusetts	MA	Boston
Michigan	MI	Lansing
Minnesota	MN	Saint Paul
Mississippi	MS	Jackson
Missouri	MO	Jefferson City

State	Postal Abbreviation	Capital
Montana	MT	Helena
Nebraska	NE	Lincoln
Nevada	NV	Carson City
New Hampshire	NH	Concord
New Jersey	NJ	Trenton
New Mexico	NM	Santa Fe
New York	NY	Albany
North Carolina	NC	Raleigh
North Dakota	ND	Bismarck
Ohio	OH	Columbus
Oklahoma	OK	Oklahoma City
Oregon	OR	Salem
Pennsylvania	PA	Harrisburg
Rhode Island	RI	Providence
South Carolina	SC	Columbia
South Dakota	SD	Pierre
Tennessee	TN	Nashville
Texas	TX	Austin
Utah	UT	Salt Lake City
Vermont	VT	Montpelier
Virginia	VA	Richmond
Washington	WA	Olympia
West Virginia	WV	Charleston
Wisconsin	WI	Madison
Wyoming	WY	Cheyenne

Skills Index for *Exploring American History 2*

READING

Comprehension

Critical Thinking

Literary Content

Skills

WRITING

Answer Key to Test-Taking Workshops

Workshop II *(pages 27–28)*

S1. C
S2. D

1. B
2. A
3. D
4. A

Workshop IV *(pages 55–56)*

S1. D
S2. B
S3. D
S4. A

1. B
2. C
3. D
4. A
5. D
6. A
7. B
8. C
9. A

Workshop VI *(pages 83–84)*

S1. C
S2. D

1. B
2. A
3. B
4. A

Workshop VIII *(pages 111–112)*

S1. D
S2. A

1. D
2. C
3. B
4. B
5. C
6. A